A Place in the Sun

A Place in the Sun

Buying Your Dream Home Abroad

Fanny Blake

Introduction by Amanda Lamb

First published in 2001 by Channel 4 Books, an imprint of Pan Macmillan Ltd, Pan Macmillan, 20 New Wharf Road, London N1 9RR, Basingstoke and Oxford.

Associated companies throughout the world

www.panmacmillan.com

ISBN 0 7522 2001 2

Introduction © Amanda Lamb, 2001
Text © Fanny Blake, 2001

9 8 7 6 5 4 3 2 1

A CIP catalogue record for this book is available from the British Library.

Design by Perfect Bound Ltd
Maps created by ML Design
Colour reproduction by Speedscan
Printed and bound in Great Britain by Bath Press

Thanks to Trevor Bennett and John Howell for their assistance with the property-buying guides.

The information given in the climate charts is taken from www.weatherbase.com. The information in the fact boxes is taken from www.cia.gov/cia/publications/factbook.

This book accompanies the first three series of *A Place in the Sun* made by Freeform Productions for Channel 4.
Executive producers: Ann Lavelle and Antoine Palmer
Series Producer: Stephanie Weatherill

Picture credits
7 Cindy Karp; 8 Spanish Tourist Office; 10 Spanish Tourist Office; 11 Spanish Tourist Office; 13 The Travel Library/Philip Enticknapp; 14 Spanish Tourist Office; 15 Spanish Tourist Office; 16 The Travel Library/Ch. Hermes; 17 Spanish Tourist Office; 18 The Travel Library/Stuart Black; 20 John and Fiona Simm; 21 (both) John and Fiona Simm; 22 George and Frances Phipps; 23 (top) George and Frances Phipps; 23 (bottom) Spanish Tourist Office; 24 Varinda Dhami and Steve Cox; 25 Varinda Dhami and Steve Cox; 28 The Travel Library/Stuart Black; 30 Portuguese National Tourist Office; 31 The Travel Library/Stuart Black; 32 The Travel Library/Rob Moore; 33 Portuguese National Tourist Office; 34 Portuguese National Tourist Office; 36 Joannah Middleton; 37 Portuguese National Tourist Office; 40 The Travel Library; 42 World Pictures; 43 The Travel Library; 44 The Travel Library/Stuart Black; 45 The Travel Library; 47 The Travel Library; 48 The Travel Library/John Lawrence; 50 & 51 Adam Brimley; 54 Alpine Apartments; 55 (top) Bob Camping; 55 (bottom) Alpine Apartments; 56 Susan Klugman; 57 Susan Klugman; 58 The Travel Library/Ch. Hermes; 60 World Pictures; 61 World Pictures; 62 The Travel Library/Philip Enticknapp; 63 The Travel Library/Ch. Hermes; 64 World Pictures; 66 The Travel Library/Philip Enticknapp; 67 The Best in Italy; 70 World Pictures; 72 The Travel Library/H.G. Schmidt; 74 The Travel Library; 75 The Travel Library/Steve Outram; 76 The Travel Library/Stuart Black; 78 Linda Norris; 79 Linda Norris; 80 Eurodome Hassapis; 81 Karatzas and Associates; 84 John Blencowe/Life File; 87 The Travel Library/Stuart Black; 88 The Travel Library/David Forman; 89 Travel Ink/David Cameron; 90 Su Davies/Life File; 92 Tim Levingston and Bridget Ives; 93 (both) Tim Levingston and Bridget Ives; 96 The Travel Library/Suellen Raven; 99 World Pictures; 100 ImageState; 101 World Pictures; 102 World Pictures; 104 Caron Beith; 105 Caron Beith; 108 Travel Ink/Andrew Watson; 111 World Pictures; 112 (top) World Pictures; 112 (bottom) World Pictures; 113 Chris Bradley/Axiom; 114 World Pictures; 116 Monika Stedul and James Fergusson; 117 (both) Monika Stedul and James Fergusson; 120 Arthur Jumper/Life File; 122 Chris Bradley/Axiom; 123 World Pictures; 125 Jan Suttle/Life File; 126 Peter M Wilson/Axiom; 128 Freeform; 129 Freeform; 132 Visit Florida; 134 Visit Florida; 135 Visit Florida; 136 Daytona Beach Area Convention and Visitors Bureau; 137 Visit Florida; 140 Joanna Woolf; 141 Sue and Dave Lewinton; 142 Joanna Woolf; 143 Carol and Bill Giles; 146 World Pictures; 148 The Travel Library/Stuart Black; 149 The Travel Library/Stuart Black; 151 ImageState; 152 World Pictures; 154 Peter Sullivan and Sally Turner; 155 World Pictures; 156 Deborah Robertson; 157 Island Investments.

Notes
The prices given for properties visited by house-hunters are accurate for the exchange rate at the time of the visit.

Contents

Introduction by Amanda Lamb 6

Spain and the Canary Islands 8

Why buy a property abroad? 26

Portugal 28

How to find the right property 38

France 40

Check before you buy 56

Italy 58

Relocation 68

Greece 70

Working out your budget 82

Turkey 84

Getting a mortgage 94

Cyprus 96

Building, restoring, renovating 106

Croatia 108

Leaving it all behind 118

Bulgaria and Romania 120

What can I take with me? 130

Florida 132

Making yourself at home 144

Eastern Caribbean 146

Further Reading 158

Property Exhibitions 158

Useful Addresses 159

Estate Agents 159

Introduction

Thank you for buying *A Place In The Sun*. I hope that you get a lot of pleasure from reading it. It is packed with stunning and evocative pictures, features about all the countries we have visited and plenty of practical information on buying property abroad. It's been designed to enhance your enjoyment of the show, and to inspire you to start searching for your very own place in the sun.

This has been my first time presenting *A Place In The Sun* and I have loved every minute of it. I've travelled to some remarkable places and had many unforgettable experiences. I think that the nature of the show, getting to grips with actually living in a country as opposed to just holidaying there, has enabled me to see different cultures on a deeper level, getting under people's skins and seeing how they tick. One of the main things that has struck me is how generally happy and hospitable people have been. I'm convinced it's all to do with living in a sunny climate – it's hard to be miserable when the sun is shining!

I have also met some amazing characters: a sculptor on the Greek island of Paros who lived in splendid isolation at the top of a mountain; an Auschwitz survivor at the Holocaust Memorial in Miami, who moved us all to tears; and a man in Carriacou in the Caribbean who had devoted his life to saving endangered species on the island – although trying to film with a lively monkey, two tortoises, a dog and a cat only reinforced the common adage about never working with animals!

One of my favourite parts of the job is working with the house-hunters, all of whom have different reasons for wanting to buy a home abroad. Some have dreams of spending their winter years in a perpetual summer, others are looking for somewhere safe to raise their children, while others still are simply trying to find a good investment. Many have harboured their fantasies for years, waiting for the right time to take the plunge. Helping them finally turn those dreams into realities can be so rewarding. Buying a home can be stressful at the best of times, buying one abroad, with unfamiliar and strange property laws and regulations, can be even more so.

The aim of this book, and the series, is to help guide you through the maze. It will tell you what to look out for, and some of the pitfalls to be avoided. You can also find out how some of our house-hunters have been getting on. Has the reality of living abroad matched up to their dreams, and do any of them have any regrets? Whatever your particular reasons for being interested in buying a house abroad, I wish you all the luck in the world. There are some truly wonderful properties out there just waiting to be discovered, and one of them really could be yours – a place in the sun to call your very own. Good hunting!

Amanda Lamb, June 2001

Spain
and the Canary Islands

The coast of mainland Spain and its hinterland attracts thousands of foreign residents and holidaymakers. With a wide choice of airports throughout the country, Spain is only a shortish hop from the UK. It offers clear Mediterranean waters, an agreeable climate, great sporting facilities, a relaxed lifestyle, friendly people and a fresh cuisine. Properties range from purpose-built apartments or houses in new developments with all mod cons, to run-down fincas (farmhouses) in the hills that may still be without running water or electricity. It is possible to buy into a busy, friendly expatriate community with support systems for the elderly or other English-speaking children, or to go completely native by acquiring a property in a remote village where you will eventually become part of the local community.

Off the east Mediterranean coast lie the Balearic islands, including Majorca, Menorca and Ibiza. Further south, off the coast of Africa, are the Canary Islands with their promise of year-long sunshine, dramatic scenery and plenty of beaches. From the hectic night life of Ibiza to the sleepy hilltop towns of Andalusia, from the arid volcanic landscapes of the Canaries to the lush agricultural landscape of Galicia, Spain has something to offer everyone.

Above *A typical whitewashed Spanish village nestles in the foothills of the Sierra Nevada.*

Spain is divided into 17 autonomous regions. The largest of these is Andalusia in the south, where the climate is hot in the summer and mild in winter. Its most obvious draws are its long coastline and the three remarkable cities of Córdoba, Seville and Granada. They each have their own treasures, but perhaps the most spectacular is the Moorish Alhambra Palace in Granada. Rural prosperity in the area has been improved by Spain's entry into the EU in 1986, by the establishment of an infrastructure necessary to support Seville as host for Expo '92 and by the motorways that have been built through the region linking it with Madrid and, therefore, the rest of Europe.

The smaller inland Andalusian towns have escaped the ravages of mass tourism and offer peace, simplicity and a warm welcome. The landscape is dramatic and varied – from the mountains of the Sierra Nevada and the Sierra de Grazalema in the south-west, to the deserts of Almeria in the east. Picturesque white villages cling to the side of hills beneath their church or castle, providing an attractive alternative to the busy coastal areas where property prices are more expensive.

Colour therapist and Feng Shui expert, Susan Farrar, explored the region some years ago when she had a timeshare apartment. 'What appeals to me is the light and colours, the atmosphere, the mood, the health and the Moorish history and architecture which inform all those.' She returned with her husband Terence, psychotherapist, hypnotherapist and yoga teacher, determined to find a property where they would be able to invite clients to share the magic of Andalusia. 'We want to live somewhere that is kind to the environment, with its own pure spring water, organic fruit and vegetables; and of course some guaranteed sunshine.' There is wonderful walking country around Grazalema, Ronda and the Alpujarras – across wide, open plains aflame with spring flowers, through shady cork oak forests, over mountainous terrain and along winding roads. The hillsides are laden with olive groves and other fruit and vegetable crops. Grape growers are justifiably proud of their wines, most notably the sherry that has been long associated with Jerez.

The coast of Andalusia is one of the most developed in Europe, with many golf courses and the chic resort of Marbella and its neighbours. Further east is Almeria, whose hot, dry climate supports a multitude of thriving agricultural businesses. Susan Reed and her partner, Paul Summers, came here to find a place in the sun for themselves and their baby daughter, Olivia. They felt that their money wouldn't go far enough on the more expensive Costa Blanca, but as they had read about Andalusia they were looking forward to investigating its possibilities. Almeria itself is a modern city, boasting a huge cathedral in its old quarter and the ruined Moorish Alcazaba astride the hilltop. Along the coast, there are as many as 140 beautiful, relatively uncrowded beaches lying between dramatic crags and promontories. Inland, the mountainous Sierra Cabrera resembles something from the Wild West – it is not surprising that many spaghetti westerns and *Raiders of the Lost Ark* were shot there. North of Cabo de Gata, with its excellent beaches, is Mojácar, a picturesque white-washed town a couple of kilometres inland. In the 1960s, a resourceful mayor gave land away to anyone promising to build on it. As a result, the town has changed from a run-down backwater into a smart holiday resort that has nevertheless managed to retain a genuine Spanish atmosphere.

The Costa Blanca in south-east Spain is a particular favourite of the British. The area south of Benidorm has been massively developed but it is much quieter and greener to the north where sleepy villages huddle among orange and lemon groves; the resorts of Oliva, Denia, Altea, Calpe and Javea offer more peaceful possibilities. Here, the beaches are generally less crowded, though, like the rest of the Spanish coast, nothing is at its best in July and August, when tourists arrive from all over the world. The capital of the region is Alicante, a town that has kept its charm. There are elegant esplanades,

Facts

Capital Madrid
Population 39,997,000
Land area 504,782 sq km
Currency 1 peseta (Pta) =
    100 centimos
    Euro from 2002
Electricity 220v
Time zone GMT +1 hour
Religion Roman Catholic
Language Castillian Spanish
Government Parliamentary
    monarchy

Below *Many expatriates have found Benidorm to be an Ideal location for a second home, especially given the year-round rental opportunities.*

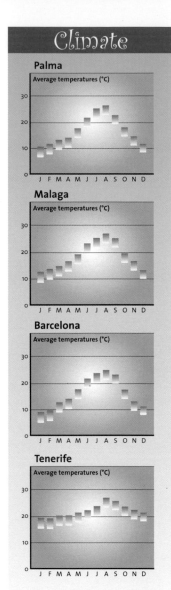

Palma
Average temperatures (°C)

J F M A M J J A S O N D

Malaga
Average temperatures (°C)

J F M A M J J A S O N D

Barcelona
Average temperatures (°C)

J F M A M J J A S O N D

Tenerife
Average temperatures (°C)

J F M A M J J A S O N D

including one along the sea front, plenty of relaxed pavement cafés and a good museum of modern art – all overlooked by the Castillo de Santa Bárbara, a 16th-century fortress that surveys the town from on high. To the south of Alicante, the old fishing village of Torrevieja has been heavily developed, with new estates constantly being built.

But as ever in Spain, if it's real quiet you're seeking, head inland. Játiva, once famous for its paper-making, is dominated by an impressive castle. Further south in the heart of magnificent mountain country is Alcoy, famed for its exciting *Fiesta de Moros y Cristianos* that takes place every April. South-west of Alicante, the land is rich in citrus trees, figs, dates and almonds. Elche is known for its palm groves, its August fiesta and mystery play, and the town of Orihuela boasts its own palm forest, three medieval churches and a gothic cathedral.

Catalonia takes up the north-east corner of Spain and exults in a wild variety of landscapes – from the mountainous north to the craggy coastline of the Costa Brava. The people are fiercely independent, speaking Catalán rather than Castillian Spanish. Their cuisine, which uses a rich variety of ingredients, is regarded as among the best in Spain. Meat and fish are plentiful – sometimes even mixed together – and many dishes are accompanied by rich sauces. The region is known for its wine production, particularly the white sparkling Cava. Catalonia is one of Europe's most significant industrial areas, much of which is centred on the region's capital, Barcelona. This is a stylish, cosmopolitan city, with extravagant architecture – including the elaborate works of the architect Gaudí – a diverse cultural diary and a busy night life. Only a one-and-a-half-hour flight from the UK, it's a perfect place for a weekend getaway.

Property in Barcelona can be expensive but care assistant and choral singer, Linda Clark, was determined to find a second home there. 'The spirit of the city came across when I was watching the 1992 Olympics. It looked beautiful and I had to come. Besides, my favourite singer, José Carreras, lives here. I came for the first time a year ago and fell in love with the city then.' A maze of narrow streets in the old city (Ciutat Vella) spreads on either side of La Rambla, Barcelona's world-famous pedestrian boulevard, which is crowded with cafés and restaurants. The gothic quarter (Barri Gòtic) is the oldest part of the city and is full of winding streets, small shops, restaurants and bars. Most of the buildings were completed before the 15th century and circle round the cathedral. In complete contrast is the waterfront Olympic Village, which was developed when Barcelona hosted the Olympics in 1992. Formerly industrial wasteland, it's now one of the most exclusive areas in the city. It lies along the foot of Montjuic, one of the seven hills around Barcelona, and is now given over to attractions such as the castle, the main Olympic sites, various museums and the Fundació Joan Miró, a gallery devoted to one of the city's greatest artists. Only 10 minutes away, you will find tranquillity in the wooded hills surrounding the city where the atmosphere has a decidedly Catalán flavour.

Stretches of open beach extend between Sitges, south of Barcelona, and Tarragona, renowned for its Roman remains. North of Barcelona, the Costa Brava extends up to the French border, containing a mix of gaudy resorts and picturesque fishing villages. But venture inland and you will find a different Catalonia altogether: stunning medieval towns such as Rupit, Lleida or Solsona.

On the north-west coast of Spain, the region of Galicia is relatively free of Moorish influences. More obvious are the legacies left by the Celts, who occupied the area for three centuries (600–300 BC). Since the ninth century, Galicia has been a focus for pilgrimages to Santiago de Compostela. Separated from the rest of Spain by mountain ranges, Galicia has a spectacular coastline that is interrupted by fjord-like rías and a fertile interior of forests and pastures watered by countless rivers cutting through it. Ancient inheritance laws have meant that the agricultural land has been chopped up into smaller and smaller holdings that are no longer big enough for machine working.

Left Sitges has attracted tourists since the 1960s and is now one of the most expensive resorts on the Costa Dorada.

The people are deeply independent and proud of their Celtic heritage, retaining many of its traditions and its distinctive language, Gallego. Their belief in magic and superstition is legendary. The food here is excellent – much of it seafood – with specialities such as octopus (*pulpo a la gallega*), orange mussels (*mejillones*) and a fish-and-potato stew (*caldeirado de pescado*). As for something to wash them down with, there are good wine labels such as Ribeiro, Condado or Albarino, beer from La Coruña (Estrella de Galicia) and a local grappa-like hooch called orujo.

The city of Santiago de Compostela is world-renowned for its medieval shrine of St James. Perhaps, though, a greater attraction for the house-hunter would be the northern coast (or Rías Altas) with its busy port of La Coruña; many good beaches; numerous unspoilt towns and villages such as Vivero, Ortiguero and Porto de Vares; and the medieval gems of Pontedeume and Betanzos. The western coast (Rías Bajas) has the safest beaches, which are fringed with pine forests; the most popular areas are Rías Arosa, Pontevedra and Vigo. Sheltered from the Atlantic, this is a coastline that has got rich on fishing, wine production, tourism and smuggling. The rest of the northern Spanish coastline is worth investigating, too. With a direct ferry link between Plymouth and Santander, it's easy to get to and rewarding when there. Glorious stretches of golden sand are backed by the Cordillera Cantábrica, a walker's paradise, and the towns and fishing villages have remained relatively unspoilt. In 1995, the biggest national park in Europe was created – the Parque Nacional de los Picos de Europa. It has stunning scenery, a wealth of flora and fauna, and would be a great location for an avid rambler looking for a holiday home.

Spain and the Canary Islands ·

Above *Palma is dominated by its vast gothic cathedral and the Castel de Belver.*

Balearic Islands

The three principal Balearic islands of Ibiza, Majorca and Menorca are Spain's biggest tourist attraction. The climate is Mediterranean with cool winds that blow off the sea, and beautiful beaches are lapped by warm waters. Head out of the main tourist spots and you'll find the islands have much more to offer than you would discover on a two-week package holiday.

Majorca is the largest of the Balearics and one of the most popular destinations for German and British home-buyers. With Ibiza, it was one of the original destinations for 1960s package tour holidays. As a result, the south-west of the island is heavily developed with high-rise resorts such as Magaluf, where there are hordes of tourists and English pubs. However, the rest of the island is very different as there are strict building regulations to ensure that its character is retained.

Up on the north-west coast, sheltered by the mountainous Serra de Tramuntana, there's a craggy coastline behind which are pine forests, olive groves and quiet villages built in the local stone. Small towns such as Deiá, Banyalbufar and Estallencs are well worth considering. In central Majorca, some old fincas still exist – ripe for restoration far from the madding crowd. The east coast has various resort towns developed beside the good beaches, but they are less frenetic than those in the south-west and quieter coves can still be found. Long a favourite retreat for writers and artists, the island has now found favour with the rich and famous who have luxury homes there. The capital of Majorca is Palma. Here the gothic buildings of the old quarter are being renovated

and converted into convenient town apartments. Thanks to tourism, the standard of living is high, though the island is extremely crowded during the summer.

Like Majorca, Ibiza has fine beaches and a wild coastline with an unspoilt rural interior. Ibiza first attracted the hippies in the early 1960s and is now renowned for its night life and dance clubs where foreign visitors party the night away. Needless to say, the popular resorts are not for everybody, especially in the summer. DJ John '007' Flemming was looking for a summer base where he might open a recording studio. 'I have been coming to Ibiza for nearly 10 years now with my work as a DJ. Over this time I have got to know and like the island and its culture. It seemed to make sense to have a second home there when a major part of my work takes me back and forth from the island.'

Ibiza town is a vibrant place with a vast range of bars, restaurants and clubs; as a bonus it is close to some great beaches. San Antonio, the world famous clubbers' paradise, has been so commercialised that property is cheap though you have to be pretty tolerant or an inveterate party animal to survive there. Seclusion can be found in the island's remote mountainous interior, which is the least populated part of the island. Here property is inevitably much cheaper than it is close to the coast, and you'll find tiny, attractive villages such as Sant Llorenç de Balafia and Santa Gertrudis de Fruitera hidden among olive groves and citrus trees.

Menorca boasts a more relaxed pace of life than Ibiza or Majorca. Like the other islands, it has a craggy coastline, good beaches and rolling green countryside. In 1993,

it was declared a Biosphere reserve by UNESCO to ensure the preservation of both the S'Albufera dies Grau wetlands and the archaeological sites that have been found all over the interior. As the northern island of the group, Menorca has a slightly wetter climate and generally is cooler, with the cold *trasmontana* wind blowing between October and April. Ferries from the Spanish mainland and Majorca arrive at the capital, Mahón, on the east coast. Mahón is a pleasant town with a distinctly British feel and an impressive harbour. There is a little of the old quarter to be explored but there are elegant Georgian mansions on the outskirts of the town. The Xoriguer gin distillery produces a distinctive Menorcan gin that was introduced by the English and is drunk throughout Spain. The other principal town is Ciutadella, which was the capital of the island under the Muslims, and then the Christians, until the British arrived. The island remains largely unspoilt and is popular with British homebuyers looking for a quiet retreat.

Above Ibiza town is an old walled town, which winds up the hill overlooking the harbour. Strict building regulations mean that the landscape of Ibiza has not been ruined by the high-rise blocks found in south-west Majorca.

Canary Islands

The Canary Islands consist of seven major and six tiny islands situated off the west coast of Africa. Each island has volcanic origins which result in extremely dramatic landscapes. Local cuisine derives from peasant and fishing traditions, and is simple and filling. Meat is generally served as stew, and fresh fish is always available and cooked simply. A favourite side dish is *papas arrugadas* – small boiled potatoes flavoured with a fierce chilli sauce. As for wine, dry and sweet wines are produced in Lanzarote and La Palma, and Gran Canaria is the source of a white-cane spirit rum. Mixed with a tree sap from La Gomera, it becomes *ronmiel* (rum-honey), which is drunk throughout the islands.

Tenerife is the largest island and is home to at least 54,000 expatriates. The island is dominated by Mount Teide, which forms part of a mountain range that divides the north of the island from the south. The south of the island is where most of the resorts, such as Los Christianos, Playa de las Américas or Los Gigantes, are found. It is highly developed, extremely lively and has year-round sunshine. Sales manager Robert Higgins and his partner, Heather Hedges, have bought an apartment in a new complex near Los Cristianos. 'A friend moved here 10 years ago and that was a magnet. It's a safe environment for our children, great weather, much less pressurised than England and there's something for every age group – waterparks for children, night life for teenagers and real serenity for older people – combined with first-class facilities.'

The north of the island is much lusher and greener than the south with a dramatic mountain landscape, beaches and picturesque towns rich in history. La Laguna, once the capital of all the Canaries, retains its elegant 17th- and 18th-century architecture and an authentic Spanish atmosphere. The cobbled streets of La Orotava may challenge weary legs but it is a charming colonial town. Further into the mountains, the villages become more Spanish in character and property is cheaper. The mountains offer sensational views and a delightfully cool retreat in summer.

Fuerteventura is the second largest island, almost barren in the interior but with spectacular beaches. It is the oldest of the islands and has the least dramatic scenery

because of the thousands of years of erosion by the fierce wind (*el viento fuerte*) that blows regularly. This is a landscape to love or loathe. Sparsely settled, with a skyline interrupted by windmills and churches, the interior may seem bleak but look closer and you will find small villages and the ancient capital of Betancuria founded in 1405. The northern coastal town of Corralejo is still a traditional fishing village at heart despite having become a popular resort only an hour's ferry ride from Lanzarote. Just outside Corralejo there are fabulous beaches and spectacular sand dunes. Most of the resorts are in the south of the island where the beaches, rated among the best in Europe, offer superb windsurfing and surfing. If you really want to get away from it all, this is a place to head for. After holidaying here for several years, retired film and publishing executive, Michael Grant, came house-hunting. He was completely won over by its desert-like charm and volcanic landscape. 'The lava-built houses and dry stone dykes remind me of certain parts of Scotland, the beaches are beautiful and it's wonderful for seafood. Seeing the sort of property available has made me consider moving here permanently.'

Gran Canaria offers a mix of cosmopolitan, seaside and rural attractions. The landscape and climate are infinitely variable, with lush tropical vegetation in the interior, desert sand dunes in the south and dramatic canyons in the mountain regions. The capital, Las Palmas, was once a stepping stone for the conquistadors en route to South America; now it's a mecca of restaurants, bars, theatres, art galleries, duty-free shopping and night life. The south-east of the island is most popular with British tourists because of its long stretches of beaches, such as the Playa del Inglés and Maspalomas, which are interrupted by fishing villages. The first hotel was built in San Agustín in the 1900s; now the resort's low-rise buildings and attractive gardens appeal to an older homebuyer. The north of the island is less touristy, more Spanish and much greener. Arucas is a small town dominated by its neo-gothic cathedral that was built as a sign of the region's wealth. Not far from there, Agaete is a picturesque town of leafy plazas, white houses and narrow alleyways. Its busy harbour is overlooked by a famous

Above *Puerto de la Cruz is a resort town, but it has kept its own identity thanks to the local Canarians who live and work there.*

Spain and the Canary Islands · **17**

Right Betancuria, once Fuerteventura's capital, is now a tranquil and attractive village in the centre of the island.

rock formation called Dedo de Diós (Finger of God). At the island's heart is a breathtaking mountain landscape with totem rocks marking it as a sacred area for the early Canarians, or Guanches. Retired bank manager, John Emmerson, and his wife, Patsy, visited Gran Canaria to look for a holiday home. 'It's not too far to fly to, it's got good, year-round temperatures, and while the south is quite commercialised the cooler, beautiful north is only a shortish drive away. We met a mix of nationalities there who were so welcoming, we hope we'll find somewhere suitable soon.'

Lanzarote is generally considered to be the most striking of the islands. Its extraordinary interior landscape was created over 250 years ago by a series of volcanic eruptions and, within the spectacular lunar landscape, you can still see volcanic activity. The people of Lanzarote have carefully looked after their island, banning high-rise blocks, advertising hoardings and pylons. The main tourist activity is centred on the east of the island. Arrecife is the capital, a modern town known for the Castillo de San Jorge which contains the International Museum of Modern Art and the home of César Manrique, Lanzarote's great artist. To the west of the town is Puerto del Carmen, the island's largest resort, which is built up round an old fishing port. The island is known for its whitewashed stone houses – with their green doors and shutters, and their chimneys topped with onion-shaped domes – camels, palm trees, vineyards and brilliant flowers.

La Palma, the greenest of all the islands, is also known as La Isla Verde. It produces tobacco, bananas and avocados. The stark surroundings of the capital, San Sebastian, give way to the extraordinary landscapes of the interior. Famed for its black beaches, La Palma's greatest attraction lies in its exquisite natural beauty. Reputed to be the highest island in the world, a leading observatory (El Observatorio del Roque de los Muchachos) stands on its tallest peak. The prettiest villages of the island are found in the south looking out over the ocean with pine forests as their backdrop. While the town of La Gomera has still escaped the ravages of tourism, it is attractive to foreign residents escaping from the melée sometimes to be found on the larger islands.

Exploring Spain and its islands will yield numerous different experiences and opportunities. Whether you're looking for a second home or plan to move lock stock and barrel, a bit of research and time spent looking will repay you with a place that fulfils all your dreams.

How to get there

Air
Iberia and British Airways fly direct between Heathrow or Gatwick and Alicante, Barcelona, Bilbao, Madrid, Málaga, Orviedo, Santiago de Compostela, Seville and Valencia, the Balearics and Canaries. Various charter companies also operate flights.
Flight time: 2–3 hours
Ferry
Ferries run from Plymouth and Portsmouth to Bilbao and Santander.

A Place in the Sun

How to buy property in... Spain

Buying property in Spain can be problematic but this introduction will give an idea of basic procedure. Always get a lawyer to check the contracts you are signing, preferably from a specialist firm familiar with the law of Spain and also of your own country. The title deed will have to be signed in front of a local notary (*notario*). It is not the *notario*'s job to verify the clauses or protect you against fraud, so his involvement is no substitute for independent legal advice.

Each sale varies in its detail. Your lawyer should conduct searches regarding the various aspects of the purchase, such as checking that you are buying what you think you are buying in terms of the property and surrounding land; checking that the seller has legal title to the property; checking that there are no unpaid debts accrued against the property and ascertaining whether there are any building restrictions imposed by the local authority.

Generally, when you have chosen your property, a private contract (*contrato privado de compraventa*) is drawn up, which specifies details of the buyer and seller, purchase price, deposit (usually 10 per cent), completion date, method of payment, any extras you have agreed to buy and any other relevant terms or conditions. This is a binding contract and your deposit can only be refunded under certain strict conditions. Make sure you understand what these are. It is common practice (but often foolish) for the sale and purchase price to be understated so that the seller's liability for capital gains tax is reduced. Remember, when you come to sell and the actual price is declared, you will be liable to pay the tax on the additional (paper) profit.

The purchase is usually completed up to three or four months later in front of the notary when the final deed (*escritura de compaventa*) is signed by you or by someone in whom you have invested the power of attorney. Property is sold in the condition it's in at the time of completion so it should be checked by you and/or your representative. At this point the balance of the money is due and the keys will be handed over. After signing, the notary will lodge the deed with the Land Registry to formally register the change in title. This may take up to three months, at which time Land Registry fees are due. He should also give you a copy of the deeds so that your lawyer can complete the other legal formalities. The notary's fees are set by the government and are due at completion. You should budget approximately 10 per cent of the purchase price to cover the additional taxes, Land Registry fees, notary fees and legal fees.

If you are buying 'off-plan', that is, the property is still being built, payments will be made in agreed stages. These vary according to the developer. Make sure the contract allows you to retain a final payment until 6–12 months after the building is finished so that you can recall the builder if there are any faults.

Useful Addresses

Spanish Consulate General
20 Draycott Place
London SW3 2RZ
Tel: 020 7589 8989

Spanish Embassy
24 Belgrave Square
London SW1X 8QA
Tel: 020 7235 5555

Spanish Tourist Office
22/23 Manchester Square
London W1M 5AP
Tel: 020 7486 8077

24-hour visa information service
0900 160 0123

House-hunters

'We love the Spanish, the food, the atmosphere. There's a comfort factor in returning to the same place, knowing it and making friends there.'

John and Fiona Simm

Account manager John and his wife, Fiona, a fitness instructor, wanted a second home on the Costa Blanca. 'It has an ideal climate for holidays,' explained John. 'And it's important that our two young daughters Giverny (9) and Bronte (7) will be happy so there must be things they will enjoy too.'

First they saw a three-bedroomed show house in the Montebello development at Torrevieja with a terrace and the option of their own pool – all for £77,000. It was light and spacious with a flexible layout that could be custom-designed to suit the new owner. With every modern convenience and great rental potential, it seemed ideal until they discovered a two-lane motorway was due to be constructed close by.

Their next possibility was an unmodernised house in Pedreguer set among orange, lemon and almond groves. For £79,000 it even came with a garage and a car. It was a big renovation project that needed an architect's report on the structure and the termite activity in the woodwork. Fiona felt the property had lots of potential but in the end they agreed it would involve too much work.

The northern Costa Blanca has some of the best golf courses in Spain so when John, a keen golfer, saw the £81,000 two-bedroomed show house in the Campoamor complex he was in seventh heaven. The house had great views and access to all the facilities on the complex including the swimming pool, tennis courts and golf course. Fiona was less sure, pointing out that the pool was too far from the house for her to feel comfortable about the children going there alone.

Below John and Fiona fell in love with their villa as soon as they saw it.

Finally they looked at a three-bedroomed villa in the hills behind Javea. In a protected area with its own pool, this definitely had the 'wow' factor. 'How could you not love it?' asked Fiona. 'It's tastefully decorated and would suit all the needs of the family with plenty of room for the children and guests.'

However, the next day they saw a £112,000 two-bedroomed villa with its own pool close to the property they'd viewed in Pedreguer. Within two minutes of walking onto the terrace they'd decided to buy. 'We're in a national park where it's quiet and peaceful with stunning views, but Denia and Javea are nearby. We're planning on converting the under-build to give us another two bedrooms.' On a hill overlooking La Sella Golf Course, the villa shares all the amenities of the golfing village – communal swimming pools, stables, tennis courts, a small supermarket and a chemist. Buying the property presented no problems. Their estate agent talked them through the process and the notary went through the con-

tracts with them and the other interested parties to double-check and triple-check that they understood everything before signing the *escritura*. 'The local councils promote and encourage "black" money,' explains John. 'By declaring a lower property value on the official records they pay less capital gains tax. A large amount of cash was handed over when the contract was signed.' John quickly realised it was better not to accept the initial mortgage terms offered by a Spanish bank. He immediately investigated what else was available and then bartered the rate down. 'We've got a fixed mortgage at two years for 5 per cent and they reduced the bank charges.' They intend to spend most of the school holidays in their new home, renting it to friends and family for the rest of the time. Any regrets?

Above and below A pool was an essential for the Simms family, but they hadn't expected to find one with such a splendid view.

'None. We love the Spanish, the food, the atmosphere. There's a comfort factor in returning to the same place, knowing it and making friends there. We're all learning Spanish so we can mix more easily with our Spanish neighbours and I think that will be a benefit to the girls when they get older too. The advice I'd give anyone would be: just do it – it's wonderful.'

House-hunters

'I really like it busy and buzzy. I won't need a car because everything's in walking distance and it was great to find somewhere we'll be able to move straight into.'

George and Frances Phipps

George and Frances decided to uproot themselves and move abroad with their three-year-old daughter, Lillie-Mae, leaving their London home to their son, Joey. They were after the year-round sun of the popular Costa del Sol. Ideally, they wanted an 'absolute bargain' near the coast, although they were aware they might have to look inland if they were going to stick to their budget of £90,000. They had been out once before to look but had drawn a blank; this time they were luckier.

First, they looked at a two-bedroomed show house in the new development of Casas Majorquinas in the western part of the Costa del Sol. It was very spacious and bright with good-sized rooms and a large terrace. As with all new developments in the region, it came with a 10-year guarantee to give the new owners peace of mind. Although they were tempted, Frances felt that it was too far away from the main resorts and wanted to see what else was available.

Inland, known as 'the biosphere' because of its unpolluted atmosphere, they saw a delightful five-bedroomed village house, on the market at £83,500, in Istán in the Sierra Nevada. It was unusual in that it had plenty of private outdoor space with a roof terrace, a sun balcony and a terrace that looked across at the mountains. 'We liked the spacious outside and it was much bigger inside than it looked. It was very quaint but not really what we were looking for.' Twenty minutes from the resorts, it was too remote and too Spanish for George and Frances.

Staying inland, they saw a two-bedroomed detached villa in La Cala de Mijas, between Fuengirola and Málaga for £87,000 and only a short walk along a dried river

Right *George, Frances, Joey and Lillie-Mae.*

bed to the beach. George was tempted by the space and the friendly atmosphere but Frances was adamant that they were not going to move into anywhere that needed work even if George promised to do it – they'd done that once too often back home.

Finally, in complete contrast, they saw a new two-bedroomed apartment for £87,000 in a development close to Puerto Banus, which has a glamorous and busy marina. Complete with two marble bathrooms, a fully-fitted kitchen, a large living room, underground parking, a communal pool and a view of La Concha in the distance, it offered everything the couple wanted. 'I really like it busy and buzzy,' says Frances. 'I won't need a car because everything's in walking distance and it was great to find somewhere we'll be able to move straight into.' By the time they got home the drop in the exchange rate meant that the flat cost them £93,000 plus 10 per cent for solicitors' costs and taxes. Having paid a deposit of £2,000 plus a further 12 per cent within the following four weeks, they had to wait until the property was ready before completing the contract. 'Our estate agent, Carlos Mason of Viva Estates, made the job much easier by putting us in touch with some solicitors. We didn't have a clue who to go to. They have power of attorney and have kept us informed by e-mail. It's been so easy.'

Once they've moved there, Frances and George look forward to spending more time with Lillie-Mae, who will be enrolled in the local Spanish school, probably moving to one of the international schools when she reaches secondary school age. George has plans to continue working as a kitchen fitter while Frances wants to carry on with her work as a beautician. Neither of them have any qualms about making new friends and integrating into the local community. 'If you're going to move there, you've got to try and speak Spanish and involve yourself. In the long term, I think we'll be far better off if we can mix with both the Spanish and other expatriates. We waited a long time for Lillie-Mae, so she's precious and this will be a much nicer way of life for her.'

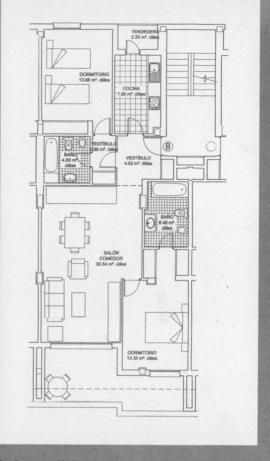

Above The plans show how the spacious living area and master bedroom will open on to a sizeable terrace.

Left The upmarket marina at Puerto Banus, lively playground of the rich and famous, is only a bus ride from the town of Marbella.

House-hunters

Varinder Dhami and Steve Cox

Holidaying in Lanzarote convinced entertainers, Varinder and Steve , that they wanted a second home there. 'It's not as commercial as Gran Canaria or Tenerife and has a character of its own. The influence of the artist Cesar Manrique is overwhelming. His presence is magnetic and he's made a real difference to the quality of the island. It's close enough to get there easily from the UK, has year-round sun and rental value and it's a beautiful place with a lot of art and culture that's been lost on the other islands.' Steve and Varinder plan to spend the first three months of the year here, renting the property for the rest of the time. They had a budget of £50,000 in cash but could raise a mortgage of £150,000.

They loved the location of a £53,000 one-bedroomed apartment in a quiet but sought-after complex near Puerto del Carmen but they felt the flat was too small. Next, they saw a two-bedroomed flat in Haria, a typical Canarian village. Its two special features were a rock wall in the bathroom and sensational views of the sea and the mountains. This was a good property in one of the prettiest valleys on the island and there was potential to extend it by buying the apartment next door, but Steve and Varinder were not tempted. The living room was dark and the location was too remote.

Below Villa complexes such as the one Varinda and Steve chose offer a range of on-the-spot facilities and good rental potential.

Left *Varinda and Steve made an offer on this stunning three-bedroomed villa.*

A villa designed by a pupil of Cesar Manrique was much more to their liking Situated in Teguise and selling for £136,000, it was a protected building with three bedrooms, a spacious living room, a stylish kitchen-diner and a cactus garden. However, it did need a bit of attention. 'As soon as we walked through the gate, we loved it. It's fantastic, a piece of history in the making.' Ultimately, realising that the rental potential was limited by its location, their heads ruled their hearts and they didn't make an offer. Three miles from Arrecife, a three-bedroomed restored fisherman's cottage was on the market for £164,000. The property had uninterrupted views out to sea and a real Canarian feel. Unfortunately, when Steve and Varinder added in the hidden costs, the price rose way over their budget.

On their next trip to the island they found what they were looking for – a semi-detached, three-bedroomed house with its own pool which was part of a development five minutes from Puerto del Carmen. But having had their offer of £120,000 accepted, things began to go wrong. 'We went to a solicitor recommended by one of the estate agents. He looked at the contract and said it was dubious because it said the vendor could hold the 10 per cent deposit until the exchange date and then say the house had been sold to someone else. He said he'd arrange another contract without that clause.' Their solicitor continually asked for the relevant paperwork from the vendor but nothing was forthcoming except demands for payment of the deposit.

'Eventually he was told it had been sold on three times even before we came on the scene. Then we heard they'd accepted another offer. Our solicitor thinks we had a lucky escape because the title deeds seem not to have been registered and the vendor couldn't provide proof the property was his to sell. It may have been a tax scam which would have left us with a hefty bill.'

The couple remain undaunted and plan another house-hunting trip soon. 'I'd love a Canarian farmhouse,' admits Varinder. 'But they're so expensive. I just wish we'd bought 10 years ago when we started talking about it.'

'It's close enough to get there easily from the UK, has year-round sun and rental value and it's a beautiful place with a lot of art and culture.'

Why buy a property abroad?

Who has not dreamed of waking every day to guaranteed blue skies and sunshine, believing that with the better weather will come a more relaxed way of life. But will living in the place of your dreams really be like an extended holiday? Stop and think. Before you begin to investigate the possibilities of moving abroad, it's essential to question your motives for doing so. You will be embarking on a substantial undertaking, both financial and emotional, so you should weigh up the pros and cons carefully, and enter into the adventure with your eyes wide open. If you're as aware of the potential disadvantages as of the advantages, you will be equipped to cope with them and be free to enjoy your move.

What are you asking of your dream home abroad? Is it a second home that you will visit as often as you can? Or a holiday home where you might stay every six months and benefit from a rental income for the rest of the year? Are you looking for a place to retire to permanently? Or do you dream of an escape from the drudgery of everyday life in the UK that will provide you and your family with renewed quality of life? Will this be the place from which you will set up a business and a new life? Know exactly what it is you want from your new home because that will help you choose the right location.

The advantages of living abroad, permanently or temporarily, may seem obvious. First of all, there's the possibility of a warmer, more friendly, climate. Then there's the attraction of a different lifestyle that may be more relaxed and stress free. Fresh local food and drink may well provide you with a healthier and cheaper diet. A move abroad, whether permanent or part-time, will enable you to experience another lifestyle, and involve you in a new and completely different environment and culture. If you plan to move to one of the capital cities, you will have the benefits and pleasures of particular sights, galleries and museums on your doorstep.

Moving abroad with young children may give you the opportunity to bring them up in a way you feel they will benefit from more than if you stayed in Britain. Living in the sun by the sea or inland in a small town may afford them a freedom in a healthy and child-friendly environment that they wouldn't otherwise have. It may be that you can choose to live in a way that will also enable you to spend more time with them.

Living abroad may well offer you the opportunity to widen your horizons and embrace new experiences. Abandoning a regular nine-to five job in favour of starting something completely different, such as running a *gîte* in France, a bar or even an alternative-therapy centre, may not bring you instant cash or relaxation; but it can be stimulating and rewarding as you set out on a path towards a new way of life that will support at least a modest lifestyle. With so many sophisticated communication systems, it may even be possible for you to continue your current work from your new property with occasional trips back home for essential meetings, as charter flights have meant that the world is ever more accessible.

If you decide to go down the route of buying and renovating an old house, you may realise your own potential in a way you had never dreamed. It will be your opportunity to design a home in exactly the way you want, experimenting with colour schemes and furniture. The experience may test relationships to the limits but it will bring tremendous rewards. A new landscape, whether rural, coastal, mountainous or a different city will be immediately invigorating and stimulating. There is the possibility of learning a new language and communicating properly with people of another culture, not to mention taking up new interests. This presents an opportunity to re-invent yourself and re-establish your family relationships when different members come to stay.

For people approaching retirement, living abroad can offer a healthy, warm climate, a welcome alternative to the British winter. Near the resort towns of Spain, Florida and Portugal, there are golf courses galore. The new developments, particularly, offer the possibility of being with other like-minded people in an environment that has the important support systems laid on to make life easier.

But have you really thought what you will be taking on? If you are not careful, a second home can be a headache. Maintaining it properly is as important as maintaining your first home. Security is another consideration. Empty holiday homes are a sitting target for burglars so it is vital that

There's the attraction of a different lifestyle that may be more relaxed and stress free; fresh local food and drink may well provide you with a healthier and cheaper diet.

nothing valuable is left inside them. You will have to find a reliable maintenance agency to look after these aspects. If you are not on the spot, you may need to appoint a local lawyer to handle the payment of any relevant taxes and bills. If you tie up your capital in a second home, you will probably forfeit opportunities to travel elsewhere. Are you sure you want to be tied down to one place?

If you are contemplating moving abroad permanently, think carefully about what you will be giving up. Perhaps the most important of these is your friends and family. No doubt they will visit you but a concentrated burst of a week or two is not the same as having people you are fond of nearby all the time. It will take time to build up a similar network in a new country. Living abroad isn't necessarily a bed of roses. If you don't get involved in the local community – it's difficult if you don't speak the language – you will be reliant on other expatriates, a much smaller pool in which to find friends. You will have to work at establishing a new set of support systems. If you are thinking about retiring abroad, you must face the realities of growing older and the difficulties of dealing with doctors in a foreign language. Its also worth bearing in mind that many countries operate a healthcare service that, unlike the NHS, is not free.

Make sure you can afford this major capital investment. Think ahead to work out where your money will be coming from to pay the mortgage and other associated costs. Don't expect to make a quick return if you sell the property or if you rent it immediately. Prices in other countries fluctuate and you may need to wait some time before you're assured of a profit. In the first place it's wise to view your purchase as something that adds to your family's happiness; any financial gain should be a secondary consideration.

Thought about it? Taken the cons on board with the pros and not discouraged? Then go for it. You're embarking on the adventure of a lifetime.

Portugal

A country rich in cultural and historical diversity, Portugal is a land where the old ways of life co-exist alongside the new. The sophisticated developments of both Lisbon on the west coast and the Algarve in the south, are culturally light years away from the tiny inland villages that seem untouched by the last century. But it is this engaging mix that draws visitors to the country. Until 1974, the country was run for 48 years by a dictatorship led by Antonio de Oliveira Salazar. The Carnation Revolution brought his rule to an end and, in 1976, the first democratically elected government came into power. Subsequent entry to the EU has helped direct Portugal towards the 21st century, with the modernisation of life in the town and country, and major investment in motorways to facilitate communications throughout the country.

Situated on the far western edge of mainland Europe, Portugal enjoys a temperate climate all year round. There are over 800 kilometres of Atlantic coastline, and Portuguese territories include the islands of Madeira and the Azores. The valley of the River Tagus (Rio Tejo) divides the rugged, mountainous north, with its landscape of forests and river valleys, from the undulating plains of the south. If you like the sun and a gentle pace of life, then Portugal may be the place for you.

Portugal has a long, seafaring history. The Portuguese have relied on their fishing industry for centuries but they were also well placed for exploration of the New World, with its opportunities for opening new trade routes. The country was also subject to invasion from other cultures. In the south, the influence of five centuries of Moorish occupation is evident: in the local architecture with its white-washed exteriors; the twisted chimneys of the Algarve; the *azulejos* or brightly glazed tiles that are everywhere; and the citrus, almond and fig trees.

The Portuguese are a welcoming people, who have a long history of good relations with the British. Traditional costume and customs are still important in the more remote areas, particularly on feast days. The Portuguese diet is characterised by seafood, particularly *bacalhao*, the salted cod first brought home by 16th-century fishermen who preserved it so it would survive the journey. Grilled sardines are also popular and their sizzling smell wafts down many a street. Among the best-known dishes are *arroz de marisco* (seafood paella), *caldeirada* (fish stew) and *cataplana* (a combination of shellfish and stew). Portugal is a successful wine-producing nation, famed for the port wine trade established in the north. There are a number of local labels from other regions – perhaps the most well-known are Dão and Mateus Rose.

The most popular areas for British homebuyers are the Algarve and the capital, Lisbon, with its adjoining coastline. Although the Algarve faces the Atlantic, it is Mediterranean in feel. The sea is warmer than on the north-west coast, and the beaches are sun-kissed stretches of sand, fringed with fishing villages and tourist developments. The 1980s saw a tourist boom that led to some hideous building developments. However, the government have since not only introduced stringent regulations to monitor what is currently being planned, but have also revoked some planning applications that had been previously granted.

Below The Algarve's recorded average of 300 days of sunshine means year-round golf on the manicured courses that have developed there.

The rugged and scenic western Algarve attracts the wealthier house-hunters. It has the most dramatic beaches, the best weather and is sheltered by the Serra de Monchique. The main town of Lagos is full of history. The first slave market in Europe was held in the Praça da República and, over 600 years ago, ships sailed from here to trade with Africa and the West Indies. The town was flattened in the 1755 earthquake, with only the fort and part of the city wall remaining intact. The narrow cobbled streets of the old town are alive with shops, cafés, bars and restaurants. Apart from the beach in the main town, there are plenty of coves tucked into the ochre cliffs just to the west. There are many fine beaches between Lagos and Sagres, the best known being Praia da Luz with its cosmopolitan atmosphere and easy-going lifestyle. On the wildest, windswept, most western point of Portugal is Sagres, once home to Henry the Navigator's school of navigation, but today little more than a white-walled fishing village whose focal point is its lively harbour.

The whole of the western Algarve is less developed than the east, and there are more traditional and country houses to be found here. Jenni Seaton, a receptionist at a leisure centre, and her husband, Bob, a freelance TV commercials director, were bowled over by the area when they first visited. 'As we travelled west from the busy cosmopolitan town of Lagos, we discovered large agricultural areas with sparse buildings, bordered by an unspoilt coastline with empty sandy beaches, not unlike the north of Cornwall – but with sun. We're intending to move to the area as soon as our UK affairs permit, and Bob will continue with his work from there while I will look for work as a fitness instructor or travel rep.'

Away from the coast, sleepy, whitewashed villages doze in the sun, including Caldas de Monchique, known for its spa water, and the nearby market town of Monchique, surrounded by wooded hills.

Central and Eastern Algarve are quite different. This is the part of the coastline which attracts swarms of tourists and a good number of expatriate homebuyers. The coast has been colonised by tourism since the 1980s, with fishing villages given over to tourist demands and a number of independent resort villages springing up between them. The most established purpose-built holiday estate, which caters for residents and tourists, is the prestigious Vale do Lobo. Moorish-influenced architecture complete with tennis courts, golf courses and other sporting facilities, shops, restaurants and discos provide a little bit of paradise for the less adventurous. However, if you want to find the real Portugal, you only have to cross the N125 highway and go a short distance inland. Loulé, a former Roman and Moorish settlement, is renowned for its lively market, its handicrafts, its high-spirited carnival in early spring and the religious festival of *Nossa Senhora da Piedade* just after Easter. Silves is a quiet little town with its impressive Moorish past visible in the remains of the mighty, red brick fortress that dominates the surrounding orange, lemon and almond groves below. The convenience of Faro airport makes London only a three-hour flight away. Faro is the capital of the Algarve. Though

Facts

Capital Lisbon
Population 10,048,000
Land area 92,391 sq km
Currency 1 Portuguese escudo
(Esc) = 100 centavos
Euro from 2002
Electricity 220v
Time zone GMT
Religion Predominantly Roman
Catholic
Language Portuguese
Government Parliamentary
democracy

Below Only three hours from London, Faro's old quarter has great potential for the British homebuyer.

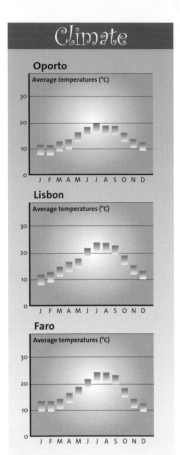

Oporto
Average temperatures (°C)

Lisbon
Average temperatures (°C)

Faro
Average temperatures (°C)

most of it was destroyed by the earthquakes of 1722 and 1755, there is a charming old quarter, the *cidade velja*, several interesting churches and pleasant harbour gardens. The coast east of Faro is less crowded. It is fronted by the Parque Natural da Ria Formosa, which is made up of a chain of saltpans, lagoons and islands, which have become a watering hole for migratory birds en route elsewhere. Property prices tend to be cheaper here but, in all likelihood, not for long.

In contrast, the capital city of Lisbon is a sophisticated metropolis. Although the country's economy has at times struggled to cope with the influx of colonials repatriating themselves as the old Portuguese empire crumbled, the reassimilation of these so-called *ritornados* has added much to the excitement and colour of contemporary Lisbon life. The seven hills on which the city is built are easily negotiated using the old trams or funicular railways that work the streets. Although much of the original city was destroyed by the 1755 earthquake, the warren-like Alfama, the old Moorish quarter with its castle perched up high, is a colourful, busy area which combines both traditional and modern ways of life. Similarly, the Baixa district has nostalgic street names dedicated to different trades, though today's reality is a busy district humming with shops, restaurants and banks.

The city is only a half-hour train ride from the resort towns of Cascais and Estoril, which have been attracting tourists since the 19th century. No longer a sleepy fishing village, Cascais has a charming old town, where there's still a fabulous fish market, with twisting cobbled streets that you can explore away from the crowds. The casino and

Right *The busy beach resort of Cascais still retains much of its original, old-world atmosphere.*

the golf courses are Estoril's main resort attractions. Other towns and villages around Lisbon are also worth exploring. These include Sintra, well known for its 14th-century palace, Setúbal with its wonderful beaches and fish restaurants, and the fishing village of Sesimbra at the edge of the Parque Natural da Arrábida.

Above The old spa town of Castelo de Vide in the Alentejo has retained its authentic Portuguese flavour.

The plains of Baixo (lower) and Alto (higher) Alentejo stretch northwards from the Algarve, edged on the east by the craggy skyline bordering Spain, and on the west by the Atlantic. Only a couple of hours drive from the busy Algarve, this is one of the most beautiful regions of Portugal, with cork oak forests, olive groves, Moorish castles and tiny villages interspersed with rivers and lakes. Unlike northern Portugal, where farming historically consisted of smallholdings, the landscape here is dominated by vast agricultural estates that stretch for miles. The main attractions of the region are Évora, situated in the more scenic Alto Alentejo, and the fortified towns of Elvas and Estremoz which, like Borba and Vila Viçosa, are known as 'marble towns' because of the nearby quarries. Megalithic stone circles, boulders and stone tombs crop up all over the plains as reminders of its distant history.

The second largest city in Portugal is Oporto (known to the Portuguese as Porto), built on the hillsides overlooking the mouth of the river Douro. The Ribeira district, on the edge of the Douro, is the most atmospheric quarter with its cobbled streets and quay-side restaurants and cafés. Far from being solely devoted to tourists, Oporto has a daily vegetable market that takes place against the backdrop of local people going about their everyday business. The almost Dickensian 19th-century streets scramble higgledy piggledy up the hill from the riverside towards the modern town. As European City of Culture for 2001, Porto received a facelift that has included the restoration of the historical areas. The beaches close to the town are polluted, but just a little to the north are more pleasant resorts and the beaches of Minho. On the bank of the Douro is Vila Nova de Gaia, which is connected to Porto by five bridges and is home to the historic

How to get there

Air
British Airways and TAP Air Portugal fly from Gatwick and Heathrow to Lisbon, Faro and Oporto. Air Portugala fly from Manchester to Lisbon, Faro and Oporto. Various charter airlines operate flights to Lisbon and Faro.
Flight time: 2–3 hours

port wine lodges. In the 19th century, the Marques de Pombal demarcated the areas on the banks of the Douro where the grapes for legitimate port wine would be grown.

The real attraction of the region is the Douro valley itself. On either side, as you travel up the valley, are terraced slopes for the growth of port wine grapes. The craggy and spectacular countryside is interrupted by various picturesque old towns such as Vila Nova de Foz Côa, close to the extraordinary rock art in the Vale do Côa (now a UNESCO World Heritage Site); and Barca de Alva, which appears untouched by progress in the mountainous border region, and has now been made part of the Parque Natural do Douro Internaçional.

Lamego is a more wealthy town, graced with elegant farms and villas on its hillside. It is linked to Peso da Régua by a winding road first built in the 18th century. Famed for its production of Raposeira, a delicate sparkling wine, Lamego is known particularly for its elegant 16th- and 17th-century mansions and the superb Baroque stairway of the Igreja de Nossa Senhora dos Remedios. This is a major pilgrimage site and is host to a Catholic festival that lasts for several weeks from the middle of August. It culminates in a parade of ox-drawn carts carrying religious scenes and the ascent to the church by the faithful.

Prices are rising in the more popular areas of Portugal but if you search further afield, real bargains can be found. However, remote regions are poorly serviced by road and rail, and housing can be fairly primitive. While you may not be daunted by the amount of work required to bring a property up to the standard you require, you may find that labour is harder to find and of a lesser quality than in the busier areas, where the service infrastructure has been better developed.

How to buy property in... Portugal

Before you buy a property in Portugal, confirm with the Land Registry office, the Conservatorio do Registo Predial, that it is registered in the vendor's name. If the property has not been passed on through a will, then a whole family may be entitled to a share of it. You will not be pleased when a distant relative appears claiming his portion.

The process of buying property in Portugal is well-regulated but is subject to change, so you will need to appoint a lawyer who understands UK and Portuguese law to check the procedure for you many people buying property in Portugal do so through an 'offshore' (tax haven) company. There are advantages to doing this, so seek advice. If you do buy in this way, the procedure will be different from that described below. Generally, however, there are two stages to go through.

The first stage is the drawing up of a preliminary contract (*Contrato Promesso de Compra e Venda*). This is binding to both buyer and seller, and is drawn by the seller's representative. It contains a description of the property; confirmation of the identities of both buyer and seller, the completion date, and the 'clear title' of ownership; and the deposit agreement. Before signing, the seller should produce all the relevant paperwork for your solicitor to check, including a habitation licence (if the property was built after 1951) and the *cardetta*, which confirms that all debts on the property are paid. A deposit of 10 per cent of the purchase price is payable by the buyer on signature of this agreement. If the buyer subsequently withdraws, then the deposit is forfeited, whereas if the seller withdraws, he will be liable to pay double the deposit.

At this stage the buyer must import the necessary funds to pay for the property, plus extra related costs such as legal fees (about 2 per cent of the purchase price) if this is paid by the buyer, not the seller, notary's fee, estate agents' commission (about 6 per cent), Land Registry fees (about 6 per cent) and property transfer tax, SISA (about 10 per cent), depending on the price of the property. If the buyer has an offshore mortgage, he will be exempt from paying SISA. He will need a *Boletim de Autorizaçao de Capitais Privados* (BAICP) from the Bank of Portugal, which gives him licence to import those funds. If he bypasses this step, he will possibly have difficulty selling the property – at least legally.

The second stage of the purchase is the conveyance (*escritura*), which is signed by both the buyer and seller (or their lawyers) in the presence of a notary *(notario)* after he has read the contract aloud to them both. The notary will want to see copies of the promissory contract, the BAICP, the buyer's habitation licence and the SISA receipt. The balance of the money due must be passed over at this stage and then the property will be transferred into the name of the buyer.

There are two other procedures for which the buyer is responsible. He must arrange registration first with the Land Registry (*Conservatória do Registo Predial*) by submitting a copy of the *escritura* to provide conclusive proof of ownership, and then with the Inland Revenue (*Repartiçao de Finanças*) for eventual payment of rates and taxes on the property.

Useful Addresses

Portuguese Consulate General
62 Brompton Road
London SW3 1BJ
Tel: 020 7581 8722

Portuguese Embassy
11 Belgrave Square
London SW1X 8PP
Tel: 020 7235 5331

Portuguese National Tourist Office
22/25a Sackville Street
London W1X 1DE
Tel: 0906 364 0610

Visa information service
0900 160 0202
24-hour tourism information
service 0900 160 0370

House-hunter

Joannah Middleton

A four-month posting in Lisbon was enough to convince IT consultant, Joannah Middleton, that this was the city where she wanted to put down new roots. 'There's so much going on here. It's an incredibly vibrant city with something for everyone – sport, history, culture or just lying on the beach.' She wanted to find something 'small with lots of character and probably central'.

Her first port of call was in the twisting, medieval streets of the Alfama district. A two-bedroomed flat had been recently renovated and priced at £78,500. Because of its position on one of Lisbon's seven hills, it commanded terrific views of the sea and the River Tagus. Another plus was that government subsidies are available for the upkeep and repair of the exterior of houses in historic districts. But Joannah felt that it was too small and dark for her, and she was keen to look at something else.

Lapa is quite an expensive district, home to the Portuguese parliamentary buildings, museums and art galleries. A self-contained flat in a quiet, narrow street was priced at £59,000. It had no particular views but it was in a smart location and had a lot of potential, even if it was on the small side. Although Joannah might not see much capital growth by buying in a popular area, the property was near the university with good rental potential. However, Joannah thought it was too small for her.

Next she ventured out of Lisbon to the sandy beaches and busy marina of nearby Cascais. A new beachside development offered an £86,000 apartment with a huge veranda and wonderful views, plus a swimming pool, tennis courts, shops and concièrge. But despite the amazing facilities, Joannah still longed for the character and culture of Lisbon itself.

The last property she saw was in the Barrio Alto district, the trendiest part of the city, full of stylish street cafés, clothes shops and restaurants. This was a recently renovated two-bedroomed loft apartment with secured views as it was in a protected area. Joannah felt it was just right for her and put in a bullish offer £9,000 below the asking price of £80,000. Portuguese house prices tend to include a huge margin for negotiation. It's worth offering less

Below Whatever the original significance of the wrought-iron letters over the door, they now represent 'Joannah Middleton's Gaff'.

A Place in the Sun

and being prepared to barter. To her delight it was accepted. She hired a Portuguese lawyer to check the paperwork, which was primarily dealt with by her estate agent, Bob Hughes, from West Coast Estates. He also recommended a British surveyor registered with Associação Portuguesa dos Chartered Surveyors, went to great lengths to keep Johannah informed of progress and chased up all the paperwork to ensure it was completed in time for the signing of the *escritora*. Three days before New Year's Eve 2000, the flat was hers.

However, things didn't quite work out as smoothly as planned when she flooded the downstairs neighbour's flat. 'Having to deal with a local plumber turned out to be very frustrating. Even though a friend was interpreting, it was so hard to get the full picture.' Fortunately, the leak was found outside the flat so major internal plumbing was avoided. Since then, Joannah has been arranging to rent the apartment to a Portuguese friend so that she can stay there whenever she wants. There is a thriving Association for Property Owners Abroad, 'but I tend to mix more with the Portuguese who are so warm and friendly. It seems easier to meet people here than in London.' It's early days but, so far, Joannah has no regrets.

'I tend to mix more with the Portuguese who are so warm and friendly. It seems easier to meet people here than in London.'

How to find the right property

Location, location, location is the age-old estate agents' maxim and it holds as true when you're looking abroad as it does in the UK. Having made the momentous decision to buy a property abroad, now is the time to consider exactly what it is you are looking for. The idyllic beach-front villa or mountain hideaway that you've returned to year after year may be perfect for a couple of weeks' holiday but does it really offer enough for a more permanent way of life?

Having decided on a particular country, you must carefully choose the area in which you most want to live. In the mountains or by the sea? In a busy town or a remote village? On the mainland or on an island? Look at the housing options open to you. If you buy an old house for restoration, you must be prepared for the troubles that come with it as well as the satisfaction of achieving your dream. Or you may prefer a modern house, ready to move into, which should come with structural guarantees. Alternatively, you may prefer the security and convenience of an apartment.

Then you will need to decide who is going to use the property. Is it to be a permanent home, a holiday home or an investment? Each one has different implications for your choice of location.

If you are uprooting your family permanently, make a list of all the things that are important to you. Think about the climate – what it is it like all year round and whether it will suit you. How near do you need to be to local facilities such as schools, leisure facilities for both you and your children, shops and healthcare facilities? If you are relocating to a new job, you will have to consider the distance you're prepared to travel every day. If you are moving to set up your own business, you must take into account how accessible you will need to be to colleagues and customers, both locally and from abroad.

How sociable are you going to be? It may be fantastic to spend a holiday completely removed from the world half-way up a mountain off a goat track, but will you be able to live with the isolation long term? And what about your children? They will want to make new friends and be able to see them. Equally, if you love the noise and bustle of a summer resort – how will you like it when the tourists have packed up and gone home and most of your favourite bars and restaurants have shut down out of season?

Consider how difficult or expensive it will be for the folks back home to get there. Presumably, they will see you as an easy touch for a cheap holiday so be generous about the number of bedrooms you specify – or not, if you are bent on escape. How many bathrooms will you need? And do you want a bath? They are much less common outside the UK. How big will you need your living space and kitchen to be? Living somewhere permanently will almost certainly demand more room than a holiday home. What about outside space? You may want a garden, a pool or enough space for one, or a garage. If you're considering a property sitting in acres of land, be realistic about the amount of time that will need to be devoted to it.

If you're planning on heading to the sun for your retirement years, there are additional considerations. It may be easier to make new friends if you retire to a villa complex where there are other people who enjoy the same pastimes and share your interests. This sort of arrangement will provide the infrastructure you are used to with all the necessary amenities on site. There are some sheltered housing schemes available on the continent where staff are on hand 24 hours a day.

When buying a holiday home that you want to use as often as possible, the most important consideration is the ease with which you can reach it. It will be more enjoyable to spend a few days away if they aren't sandwiched between a long flight or boat ride and hours of driving. Nor will you want to spend the first day there in a long journey to the nearest shop to stock up on provisions. Narrow your choice down to particular villages or towns you like and search within a limited radius of them.

If you are relying on rental income, you will have to take into account the property's accessibility to the main attractions of the region, to the UK or nearest airport. In a hot climate, the presence of a pool will dramatically increase the amount you can charge, so consider whether there is space for one and, if so, whether or not you will get planning permission for it. If you are hoping to rent your property out almost all year round, you will have to think about how seasonal the trade will be. Can you afford a property that will, in all likelihood, stand empty for six months of the year?

Many people opt for the security of buying within a resort complex – there are some obvious benefits. If you buy off-plan, you may be able to make your own specifications about the interior design and decoration. You will have access to all the various communal facilities such as swimming pools, tennis courts, golf courses, boating lakes, fitness centres, gardens, restaurants and bars. It will be easy for both you and your children to make new friends, perhaps arranging to return with them at the same times every year. You will be subject to a maintenance charge but this should remove all worries about the property and its surroundings while you're not there. The rental potential will be high and the security risk negligible. However, the lifestyle in such a community means it is unlikely you will mix with the local community or share that country's way of life.

When you have made these decisions, approach local estate agents in the area you have chosen, search via the internet and look in foreign property magazines or local papers. You will be able to get an idea of what's available by visiting foreign property exhibitions in the UK. If you have limited time to search yourself, either employ a home-finder agency based in the UK or line up a number of potential properties before you visit so that you use your time there well. There will be advantages and disadvantages to whatever you choose. But forearmed is forewarned; don't rush into buying the first thing you see. Be clear in your mind what you are looking for and the extent of your budget. Once you have made these decisions, you're on your way to finding the right thing.

Make a list of all the things that are important to you. Think about the climate – what it is it like all year round? How near do you need to be to such places as schools, shops and healthcare facilities?

France

From the snowy peaks of the Pyrenees to wooded river valleys in the heart of the country, from the alabaster cliffs of Normandy to the beaches of the Côte d'Azur, France presents many different faces. It is the largest country in Europe, and is bordered by sea, forest and mountain ranges. Over the centuries it has been home to many cultures, each of which has left its mark on the folklore and traditions that vary from region to region. Long a popular holiday destination for the British, it's easy to get to – either by plane, boat or train. Communications within the country are excellent and the variation in climate from region to region offers something to suit everyone. The more active should head for the Alps, where winter snowsports give way to a host of activities, such as hiking, climbing and paragliding in the summer. The south and west coastlines offer good weather and sandy beaches for sun-worshippers or families, while inland it's still possible to find idyllic out-of-the way properties where you can simply relax and enjoy the local way of life.

Everywhere, you will be able to share the French enjoyment of good food and wine. France produces over 365 cheeses and more than 700 wines. The weekly markets selling fresh local produce, which are held throughout rural France, are a delight. Whether you want a holiday home or are considering moving abroad for good, France may be exactly the place for you.

Moving abroad is a big decision. It's important to think about the kind of lifestyle you're hoping to embrace. Different regions of France offer very different attractions. Read about the areas you like and then visit them, travelling around so that you are certain that your next step on the property ladder will be right one. Many Britons have successfully moved to France, whether permanently or as a second home. You could be one of them.

The attractions of Paris, the capital city, are legion. Who wouldn't fall for them? Elegant boulevards, superb museums, breathtaking cathedrals, tiny courtyards, modernist architecture, first-class restaurants and the epitome of style. Only a train ride from London, what better place to own a *pied-à-terre*?

The city was originally founded on the Île de la Cité, which is circled by the river Seine and dominated by the magnificent cathedral of Notre Dame. The Seine effectively dissects the city. To its south is the Left Bank (*Rive Gauche*), associated with intellectual debate and left-wing philosophy. North of the Seine is the Right Bank (*Rive Droite*), where the major fashion houses are to be found behind the Louvre and the Jardin des Tuileries. Under Napoleon III, Baron Haussman, the Prefect of Paris, was charged with changing the face of Paris. The crowded medieval streets were demolished and replaced with the wide boulevards and bridges that are so familiar to us today. The two world wars and the Occupation left Paris undamaged but economically depressed. It was not until the 1960s and 1970s that redevelopment began in areas such as La Défense and Montparnasse on the outskirts of the city. Today, the city has a population of over two million and is divided into 20 arrondissements that spiral outwards, clockwise from the centre.

Getting around the city is made easy by the efficient Metro system, which is straightforward to master. Over the years, Paris has lost none of its magic. Culturally it offers everything: superb art galleries from the Pompidou Centre to the Musée d'Orsay and the Louvre; memorable architecture from IM Pei's glass pyramid at the Louvre to the Eiffel Tower and the Arc de Triomphe; and theatre and opera. The Parisians may have a reputation for stand-offishness but the expatriate community is definitely alive

Right *The majority of property for sale in Paris is apartments, which vary in price depending on the area. They are not cheap, but with the all the city has to offer right on your doorstep, they can be hard to resist.*

Left *The delightful seaside town of Honfleur is not only close to the northern French ferry ports, it is a mere 200 kilometres from the attractions of Paris.*

and kicking with films, plays and various publications catering for other languages, including English.

The café culture flourishes with bars and brasseries on almost every corner. The streets are clean and pleasant to wander through. The city is a fascinating place, the stylish centre contrasting with its historic quarters. These include the higgledy-piggledy streets of Montmartre with its artists, art galleries and restaurants and cafés galore, and the Marais, fashionable for nobles in the 16th and 17th centuries. The Marais has been renovated but it still retains its own peculiar identity. A city of romance and of dramatic contrasts, Paris is the perfect spot for a bolthole with a difference.

Normandy and Brittany are popular with many wanting to buy a home abroad. They are conveniently close to England and within easy reach of the attractions of Paris. The weather and countryside are similar to that of Kent or Sussex, while the dramatic chalk cliffs south-west of Dieppe in Normandy, have earned the name of the Alabaster Coast. The area is less well-developed than southern England and properties tend to be cheaper. This makes it an ideal place to relocate to, but as properties change hands quickly you need to move fast if you find something you like. Alan and Shirley French, both semi-retired company directors, came here to look for a smallish home they could renovate. 'We like the relaxed lifestyle in France. Shirley speaks good French and we've always found the people charming and helpful. The Normandy coastline is tremendously appealing and has the advantage of only being an overnight ferry ride from Plymouth so we wouldn't have a long drive at either end.'

The peaceful rural landscape is interrupted by picturesque towns and villages. Rouen is famous for its cathedral and medieval architecture. It is also where Joan of Arc was burned at the stake. Close by is Giverny where the Impressionist artist, Monet, lived. Both his home and the stunning gardens that he designed are open to the public. Near to the major port of Le Havre is the charming town of Honfleur, once the starting point for explorers of the New World. The sandy-beached coastline of this region has long been popular with holidaying Parisians.

Specialities of the area include butter, cheese (most notably Camembert), cider, the apple brandy Calvados, and delicious, fresh seafood. Other local dishes include *canard rouennais* (mouth-watering roast duck), *marmite dieppoise* (a dish combining

Above *A village surrounded by vineyards, such as this one in Burgundy, fulfils the dreams of many British people wanting to buy a home in France.*

fish, shellfish, leeks, cider and cream) and *tripes à la mode de Caen* (tripe with root vegetables, Calvados, cider and leeks).

Brittany is a granite outcrop on the most western point of France. Its coast is cut with inlets and rocky coves exposed to the stormy Atlantic Ocean. It has a landscape steeped in myth and is dotted with neolithic remains, the most famous being the standing stones at Carnac. This is the world of King Arthur's court, the home of Morgan le Fay and the Holy Grail. Inland, the Gulf Stream provides a climate that is ideal for growing fruit and vegetables – fabulous shellfish or fish stew (*cotriade*) may be followed by fresh melon, grapes, strawberries and pears. This is also *crêpe* country – where savoury buckwheat *galettes* can be followed by sweet pancakes galore.

Originally an independent duchy, Brittany was finally subsumed into France in 1532. The Breton people are a race of fishermen and farmers with a strong Celtic spirit. They have maintained their regional identity, particularly in *Basse Bretagne* where some Bretons still speak their native tongue, *Breiz*. Distinctive traditional costumes (broad hats and baggy pantalons for men, elaborate lace head-dresses for women) and music are evident on 'high' days and holidays. The larger towns of Vannes, Quimper and Rennes are justifiably proud of their ancient heritage, while St Malo and Roscoff provide convenient ferry links with England.

Families may be drawn towards the Atlantic seaboard further south, with its stretches of beaches lined with pine forests, because it enjoys a more temperate climate than that of Brittany and Normandy. The lures of the region range from the relaxed university city of Nantes in the north to the giant sand dune at Arcachon in the south. Living here means good weather and a low cost of living. Poitou-Charente is one of the most unspoilt parts of France where farmhouses can still be found for sale at reasonable prices, although many need considerable renovation. This was where Gary and Julie Scully began their search for a *gîte*. 'We just want to share the laid-back way of French life and be happy. We love meeting people. Julie teaches riding and I teach skiing, both of which we can do in France. I've been in the Forces for 20 years now so I'm ready to put my feet up and watch the sun go down with a glass of red wine. Our plan is to rent the property out till I can retire and then move over to an up-and-running business. '

The main towns of the area are La Rochelle, Poitiers, Angoulême and Cognac. La Rochelle is a delightful, relaxed fishing port where bicycles are provided free (for the first two hours) to those who want to explore. The surrounding beaches are unmemorable. Far better beaches are to be found a short boat ride away on the Île d'Oleron and other offshore islands. Poitiers is one of the oldest cites in France, with magnificent architecture, and just to its north is Futuroscope, the extraordinary cinematic theme park. Angoulême is famous for its paper-making, while Cognac is the place for brandy, which is exclusively produced in the various local distilleries. The cooking in the region is simple home fare that relies on fresh local produce, especially fish, cooked with cream and wine.

A Place in the Sun

The Aquitaine coast offers sandy beaches and dense pine forests. Its capital, Bordeaux, situated on the banks of the Garonne, is an elegant city with first-rate museums and a thriving university. The city is surrounded by acres of vineyards which, with Burgundy, produce some of the world's finest wines. Inland, the forests give way to the fertile agricultural landscape of Lot et Garonne. Two sisters, Christie and Jeanne Arno, came to find a family house here. 'Serendipity led us here. We wanted a house in southern France but had a feeling that Provence might be too hot, crowded and expensive. So then I picked this area with a pin, visited it and discovered that although the scenery was less dramatic, it offered great variety. We happened to be shown a house that came as close to what we wanted as anything ever would – it's quiet, beautiful and with the right accommodation – so rather than mess about, we decided to take the plunge.'

Ancient towns and villages perch on the hillsides among orchards, vineyards and fields waving with corn. This is a perfect antidote for busy working lives, a place where the pace of living is slow and the cost of living is low, offering a retreat from mainstream society. The people are warm and friendly, and the cuisine is excellent, notably its *foie gras*, *cèpes* and *escargots*. In the extreme south-west is the Pays Basque. This has a unique identity thanks to its Basque community, which extends beyond the Pyrenees to the north of Spain. The two principal towns are the capital, Bayonne, with its typically Basque buildings, and the glamorous seaside resort of Biarritz. Within easy reach of the Pyrenees, this is an area which boasts a variety of attractions, including first-class surfing at Anglet beach. If you want to be less energetic, you can watch the regional game of pelota (a cross between squash and lacrosse), and there is regular bullfighting throughout the summer.

Inland are the Dordogne (known to the French as Périgord) and Limousin. The Dordogne, Lot and Cère rivers flow through idyllic countryside and past sleepy villages on their way to the sea. You can visit the caves that were home to Neanderthal man, most notably at Lascaux. Many of the farmers abandoned the land in the 1950s, leaving cottages to be snapped up by holiday-home hunters. Look in neighbouring Limousin and you will find properties that are more reasonable than in the Dordogne. This is green and rolling agricultural land, which even boasts its own Limousin cow. It is sprinkled with picturesque châteaux and churches, and picture-postcard villages such as Aubazine, Collonges-la-Rouge and Beaulieu-sur-Dordogne. Toulouse and Bordeaux airports are about two and a half hours away but a new motorway has recently speeded up transport through the heart of the region. The people here represent the epitome of French warmth and generosity. The central town of Limoges is synonymous with fine porcelain but it also produces fine enamelware.

Further to the south-east is the region of Quercy, where dramatic, steep gorges flank the rivers Lot and Cère. Picturesque towns abound: St-Cirq Lapopie, which commands spectacular views from high above the Lot; Figeac, a peaceful riverside town; Carennac, a medieval village on the west bank of the Dordogne; and Martel, centre of the area's nut and truffle trade. Gastronomes will be tempted by game, fish and poultry – not to

Below *The charms of the Dordogne have seduced many British buyers, with the result that prices are high.*

mention truffles and other fungi. The lush countryside yields tender fruits and vegetables while the vineyards provide some of the best wines in Europe.

For something quite different, why not head to the mountains: the Pyrenees form the southern border with Spain while the Alps make up the border with Switzerland and Italy in the south-east. Of the two, the Pyrenees are less frequented but are just as rewarding in terms of fabulous mountain scenery. In summer, the high alpine meadows overlook the orchards and fields that flourish on the lower plains. Most spectacular of all is the Parc National des Pyrénées, a narrow area that encapsulates the entire region. Eagles wheel over the mountain summits and mountaineers, skiers and walkers will be in their element here. At the foot of the highest mountains, near Argelès, is the shrine of Lourdes, one of the principal pilgrimage sites in the world. Higher still is the extraordinary natural amphitheatre at the Cirque de Gavarnie. In the east, the Pyrenees roll down to the province of Languedoc-Roussillon where a Mediterranean coastline is backed by miles of vineyards. This is where Roy Jackson and Rosemary Cooper came to search for a romantic hideaway because they enjoyed 'the different types of architecture, by and large the weather, the amenities, its closeness to the Mediterranean.' The two main towns are Carcassone and Montpellier, which are famed for their ancient walled city and university respectively. Prices are still surprisingly cheap and if you locate a home wisely you can ski in the morning and relax with a swim in the sea in the afternoon.

Further inland is the region of Tarn, where management consultant, Nicholas Dwyer, and music teacher, Arhynn Descy, wanted to set up a music school. 'A number of things attracted us to France but the ones that come to mind are the wine, the cuisine and the weather. Also a major point is the lack of a stressful life in the southeast.' The weather here is fantastic but prices are much lower than in neighbouring Provence. The airports at Carcassone and Toulouse mean England is only two hours away. The principal town, Albi, is remarkable for its red bricks made from the clay of the nearby river Tarn. The artist, Toulouse-Lautrec, was a native of the town and the museum has the largest collection of his works. The cuisine of the region is rich in garlic and olive oil and its most celebrated dish is *cassoulet*. Nearer the coast, spicy dishes of fish and shellfish are popular.

The Alps run from Nice north to Austria and divide into two regions: Savoy to the north and Dauphiné in the south. Mont Blanc, the highest peak in Europe, soars above the year-round resort of Chamonix. In 1731, a prize was offered to the first person to climb the mountain. It was won by a local crystal cutter some years later, and subsequently a Swiss scientist completed the climb in his top coat. For those with nerves of steel, a cable car sweeps up to the Aiguille du Midi, a point commanding spectacular views, before running on to Courmayeur in Italy. For the faint-hearted, there's always the 11-kilometre tunnel cut through the mountain.

Skiing became fashionable after Chamonix hosted the first Winter Olympics in 1924. Since then, tourist development in the area has boomed with summer activities such as walking, cycling, paragliding and climbing becoming as popular as winter sports. Three spectacular national parks provide sanctuary for the region's wildlife and a heaven for walkers. The university town of Grenoble is the birthplace of Stendhal and home to the Monastère de Chartreuse, whose Carthusian monks still produce the famed liqueur. The spa towns of Aix-les-Bains, Thonon-les-Bains and Evian-les-Bains are renowned for their thermal baths and the quality of their spring water. Savoy was only united with France in 1860. Since then, the Savoyards have maintained a strong regional identity, including a distinctive dialect. The cooking revolves around local beef and lamb and mountain cheeses.

Provence and the Côte d'Azur are another distinctive region of France. Pine- and lavender-scented breezes embrace this playground of the rich and famous. The stretch

of beaches from Marseilles to Monaco are world renowned, as are the five main resorts of Menton, Monte Carlo, Nice, Cannes and St Tropez. In the summer they are overrun with French holidaymakers and the property isn't cheap.

Over the centuries this part of the world has been a port of call for numerous nationalities, all of whom have contributed to its diversity. Since the 19th century, travellers have been attracted by the temperate climate, the ambience and the intensity of colour and light to be found there. This is where painters such as Matisse, Cézanne and Picasso found their inspiration. Its popularity as a summer resort means that property is at a premium here. However, retreat inland, where places are less developed, and there are still affordable properties to be found, although they will be more expensive than in western France. Picture sleepy village squares, old men passing the day over a glass of pastis and the click of boules in the background. Picture purple lavender fields stretching into the distance. The weather is mostly warm and sunny except when the Mistral blows fiercely across the region for a few days in both spring and winter.

Among the appeals of the region are the picturesque hilltop villages. Gradually abandoned by the peasants who took to life in the valleys, many of the houses have been restored as holiday homes. Huge efforts have been made to preserve the traditional rural architecture: terracotta tiled roofs, beamed ceilings and red-tiled floors. In Nîmes, Arles and Orange, original Roman amphitheatres are still used for bullfighting and concerts, while north of Nîmes is the Pont du Gard, one of the finest Roman aquaducts in the world. Avignon is a lively city with roots that go back to before Roman days. Its fortunes changed when the Papacy moved here in the 14th century and built a huge palace that still stands in the city centre. The charms of Aix en Provence (the name derives from the Latin for water, *aqua)*, a thriving university city, are manifold. Fountains splash on many street corners, and the city's elegant 17th-century architecture and chic inhabitants are reminiscent of Paris.

Above *With many British airlines flying there, Nice is a convenient base from which to explore the beauties of Provence, the southern Alps and even Italy.*

Above The walled city of Avignon would be a great place to live for someone interested in French culture and history.

Generally, the inhabitants of the region have a more Latin temperament than elsewhere in France: passionate and volatile with a healthy disregard for time. Provençal is still spoken and traditional costumes are dusted off for the local fêtes. The cuisine relies on garlic, herbs and olive oil. Specialities include steaming stews *à la provençale*, *salade niçoise*, *soupe de poissons*, *bouillabaisse* and *aioli*, a distinctive garlic mayonnaise. The vineyards produce delicious wines, among them Bandol, Gigondas and Chateauneuf du Pape.

These are the principal regions that attract most British people wanting to embark on a new life in France. Of course, there is absolutely no reason why you shouldn't strike out into other areas, where you can be guaranteed that your neighbours won't be other expatriates. Inland France has much to offer. There is the splendid Romanesque architecture of Burgundy, a department rich in vineyards with a people devoted to their cuisine. Wild produce is prized: excellent charcuterie, cheeses such as Chaorce and Epoisses, rich stews and the special Bresse chickens all grace the Burgundian menu. Alsace and Lorraine share the north-east border with Germany. Being further north and inland, they don't offer such a warm climate. The people of Alsace are friendly while those from Lorraine are considered to be more reserved. However, the countryside is pleasant and produces good wines. Lorraine is home to the quiche; Alsace provides greater variety with its *choucroûte*, *foie gras* and spicy sausages. The Auvergne occupies the remote and rugged countryside of the Massif Central. Because it is difficult to reach, it has remained unspoilt and life is predominantly rural. There are stretches of meadows used for grazing cows and wonderful walks to be had through the volcanic landscape. The two regional parks, the Parc Naturel Régional du Livradois-Forez and the Parc Naturel Régionaldes Volcans d'Auvergne, make up France's largest environmentally protected area.

Before you choose the region of France where you would like to settle, take the time to travel round the country and to investigate the different ways of life to see which will suit you best. There are still numerous spots just waiting to be discovered. One thing's for sure – somewhere there will be something to suit you.

How to get there

Air
Air France, British Airways, Britair, British Midland and various charter companies fly directly from the UK to a range of destinations throughout France.
Flight time: 1–3 hours

Ferry
Ferries leave from Dover, Folkestone, Newhaven, Portsmouth, Poole, Weymouth and Plymouth to a range of ports in northern France.

Train
Eurostar leaves London Waterloo and Ashford for Paris and Lille.

A Place in the Sun

How to buy property in...
France

The sale of property is strictly regulated in France and conducted by a *notaire* (notary) The *notaire* is a government official and represents neither the buyer nor the seller. If you are in any doubt about the procedures, it would be wise to find a solicitor who can explain them to you. In any case it is sensible to take advice from a specialist lawyer who knows UK law and the law of France as there are many issues such as inheritance rights that the *notaire* will not deal with. Either ask your estate agent, who may be able to recommend one, or engage one from a specialist firm in Britain (see page 159). If you are buying a flat or a new property, then there will be variations in the procedure which your lawyer should be able to explain to you.

The *compromis de vente*, which is drawn up by the notary, is the most commonly used form of purchase agreement. It is a binding legal document recording the agreement to buy and sell between the vendor and the buyer. This document will include both parties' names, although it is advisable to include a substitution clause that allows another name to be inserted when you've investigated questions such as inheritance or taxation. The precise details of what is being sold should be spelled out. The purchase price, deposit and any additional fees will be mentioned. It will state that the vendor is not responsible for any defects in the property – so make sure you've done your homework with a surveyor before you sign. There will also be additional clauses that must be satisfied, for example, that you obtain a mortgage or that the existing mortgage will be repaid from the sale. If these are not satisfied, then your deposit will be returned. If completion doesn't go ahead and it

is your responsibility, then you will forfeit the deposit and may be liable to be sued for losses incurred by the vendor as a result. The contract will also specify a date for completion. A deposit of 5 or 10 per cent is paid to the notary who puts it into escrow (a third-party account) until completion arrives.

Remember the buyer is responsible for paying both the legal costs and taxes relating to the purchase. If you're buying a new property, the *notaire*'s fees will be between 2 and 3 per cent; there will also be tax to pay of 19.6%, though the advertised price may include this amount – check. If you've chosen something older, expect the *notaire*'s fees to be between 7 and 8 per cent of the purchase price. Also bear in mind that you will have to pay stamp duty and Land Registration fees on top of that.

The *notaire* must conduct various searches and enquiries. It is up to you and your lawyer to complete your own investigations into general planning proposals for the area. It is not the *notaire*'s responsibility, for instance, to notify you that there's a motorway planned to run right by your property. When he has completed his work he will draw up an *acte de vente* which, when signed, completes the transfer of property to you.

You will then be issued with an *attestation*, which is a certificate that proves you are the owner of the property. The title deeds stay with the *notaire* but you should be supplied with a copy within about six weeks.

Useful Addresses

French Consulate General
21 Cromwell Road
London SW7 2EN
020 7838 2000

French Embassy
58 Knightsbridge
London SW1X 7JT
Tel: 020 7201 1094

French Government Tourist Office
178 Piccadilly,
London W1V 0AL
Tel: 0906 824 4123

24-hour visa information service
0900 188 7733

Case Study

Adam Brimley and Vivienne Hawker

Adam Brimley and his partner, Vivienne (Viv) Hawker, were living and working in south London when they decided to sell up and head for France. 'I've always had a passion for France since I came here as a child,' explains Adam. 'When I met Viv, I wanted to share it with her and it was her suggestion to up sticks altogether. Opening a *gîte*'s a calculated risk but we didn't want to end up in our dotage in Eastbourne, saying, "If only..."' With a budget of £90,000 to include renovation costs, they travelled to Limousin with their two dogs and a caravan, and started searching for 'the biggest, cheapest property' they could find.

A traditional rural cottage near Pompadour in north Corrèze with three bedrooms, three barns and 22 acres was in a fantastic location. It was on the market for only £55,000 but Adam felt that the level of work needed to renovate meant it would take too long to generate income. They then looked further south near Coussac-Bonneval where they saw a two-bedroomed farmhouse with a barn and three acres for £49,000. The owner had begun renovating the property but Adam and Viv both felt there were things they would have done differently. Although very pretty it was too close to the neighbours so it got the thumbs down. On to Cornac to consider a £79,000 three-bedroomed village house with outbuildings, including a large hay barn. The first impressions were good. New windows and central heating had already been fitted and being in a village meant rentals wouldn't be entirely seasonal. However, they would have had to install a pool and Adam felt the necessary work would drain their capital too quickly. Viv felt that although the village was in a lovely location, it was too remote. Finally, they fell in love with an 18th-century red stone

Right *Five months after finding the house, Adam and Viv could at last start work on the massive renovation job.*

house in the delightful village of Collonge la Rouge. 'It was completely beautiful, a dream French house with oak beams, high ceilings, vaulted wine cellar, a perfect location.' But, at £78,500, it proved too expensive.

Above Adam and Viv spotted their farmhouse while driving around Limousin, at £41,000 it fitted perfectly their criteria of big and cheap.

Eventually, the couple bought a wrecked 1912 stone farmhouse near Figeac for £41,000. It came complete with a large attached barn, a pig house and five acres of land. 'We drove past in October [2000] and saw a *notaire*'s *A Vendre* sign. The place was empty, it was just what we wanted and we were cash buyers, but it took five months to buy. We had to wait because after one of the two brothers who owned it died, his widow had to change her marriage contract through a notary in Paris and, by law, the land had to be offered to the neighbouring farmers because it was over 4,000 square metres. We paid £50 to reduce the time that took to one month – it took three! So my advice would be, don't bother.'

At last they are ensconced in the building using their caravan as a bathroom while they renovate the pig house for themselves, and the house and barn into a four- and a six-bedroomed holiday home. 'Drivers slow to a crawl to watch us working. But once the locals realised we were moving here for good, they became much more friendly, welcoming us to the area.' As a result of their experiences, Adam and Viv have a lot of useful advice to offer: house-hunt in winter when you can see through the trees; deal with estate agents with caution; save time by looking at the outside of properties on your own before selecting those to see in more detail; and check what's included in and excluded from the price. With all this in mind they add, 'We can't recommend it highly enough. The French love people who do it themselves. It's mad – but why not?'

'It was completely beautiful, a dream French house with oak beams, high ceilings, vaulted wine cellar, a perfect location.'

House-hunter

Right *Attractive though it is, this large Savoyard farmhouse didn't meet all of Bob's criteria.*

Bob Camping

Property developer, Bob Camping, lives in London. He had frequently skied in the French Alps before deciding to buy a property near Chamonix, which he both plans to use regularly and rent out. 'The great thing about Chamonix is that it's close to Geneva airport so I can get there at weekends. It's not as expensive as some of the other resorts and there's some of the most challenging skiing in the Alps. Plus it's young and fun.' Bob had already looked at several places before he appeared on the programme. He wanted something big enough to have some development potential, and somewhere secluded, picturesque and within each reach of the slopes. However, it's a good idea to househunt here in the summer, when there's no snow to hide building faults.

> '**Chamonix is close to Geneva airport so I can get there at weekends. It's not as expensive as some of the other resorts and there's some of the most challenging skiing in the Alps.**'

He looked at four properties that might fit his requirements. First was a farmhouse in Les Coverays, an exclusive part of the Chamonix valley, 10 minutes walk from the town. It provided a modern, comfortable five-bedroomed retreat but Bob wasn't sure about the house, though he loved the garden. It was in a good area but still seemed expensive at £422,000. Second, was a four-bedroomed ski chalet (£278,000) in Les Houches. Ten minutes drive from Chamonix, this village is becoming very popular and has excellent public transport. There is good climbing and hiking in the summer and skiing for every level in the winter. The chalet had plenty of

development potential with a loft, garage and over half an acre of land. Bob was impressed, loved the situation with the views of Mont Blanc and thought it had great rental opportunities. Next he looked at a seven-bedroomed Savoyard farmhouse (£486,000) situated on a slope in Le Coupeau, 15 minutes south of Chamonix. Built in 1801, the house was very secluded and picturesque with wonderful seasoned wood on the floors and walls, and attractive old windows. Despite the amazing setting, Bob was worried that the slope might make development expensive and that the drive from Les Houches would worry him in the winter. Finally, he saw a more modern four-bedroomed mountain retreat (£208,000) in Servoze a little further along the valley. It was off the tourist trail but within easy reach of Chamonix, St Gervais and Geneva airport. Despite the superb living room and sensational views, it was too far from the main action for Bob. So, Les Houches it was.

Within days he had put in an offer of £5,000 below the asking price, which was accepted. It took from August to October 2000 for the purchase to be completed and then a further three months of renovations before Bob had his dream mountain hideaway. 'It was very straightforward. I was so lucky in the estate agent I bought it through, Antoine Terray of Alpine Apartments. He guided me through the whole process and we didn't have any hitches at all. I spent £35,000 doing the place up and used two women builders he recommended who were superb.' Then came the problem of moving his furniture from England. Having been quoted a price of £4,000 from a removal company, Bob decided to take matters into his own hands. He hired a van and brought the lot over, including a hot tub, for a total of £850. Within weeks of moving in he had a party for 22 people on his birthday. He's already made local friends through Antoine and has no doubts that following his gut instinct has led him to choose the ideal place in the French Alps.

Above top Bob's traditional alpine chalet has the benefit of being near Chamonix, both a winter and summer resort.

Above For a keen skier such as Bob, the view of Mont Blanc was impossible to resist.

House-hunter

Susan Klugman

Susan Klugman has enjoyed Paris ever since she was a student at the Sorbonne. After years of visiting friends who lived in the city, she finally took the plunge and, with their help, bought a small, inexpensive *pied-à-terre* near Bastille in the 11th arrondissement. 'I've been made to feel welcome and people have been so helpful that I now feel quite at home and have found Paris to be a very friendly city.' Susan lives in London so can be at her *maison secondaire* within four and a half hours. Forward-planning means that she can take advantage of available ticket deals on Eurostar. She has many French friends, loves the art and food and wants to keep a home in Paris. Nevertheless she is aware that the five flights of stairs may eventually become a bit much.

She went to see four flats that might suit her better. The first was in the Rue St Honoré, which is in the prestigious 1st arrondissement. Flats here tend to be small and this was no exception. It was a studio apartment on the first floor of a 17th-century building, with a galleried bedroom, living room, kitchen and bathroom. At £92,000, the price reflected the location but it did have high rental potential. However despite it being 'very unusual, in a wonderful location and beautifully decorated – a perfect *pied-à-terre*', Susan felt it was too small for her. On to the fashionable Marais where prices are slightly lower. The flat was on the fourth floor but the installation of a one-person lift was imminent. The flat was charming, with a double reception, bedroom, kitchen and bathroom. It overlooked a courtyard which allowed light to flood into the rooms. It was a better size for Susan but she found the entrance to the

Below Susan Klugman flat-hunting in Paris.

A Place in the Sun

flat daunting and the price of £118,000 seemed high. Then up to Montmartre, an area steeped in artistic history with breathtaking views of Paris. Only 10 minutes from the Gare du Nord and Eurostar, it is an extremely convenient area for British people wanting to live in Paris. Property has tended to be cheaper here, but prices are rising. For Susan the two advantages of the £108,000 flat were a private garden and a concièrge. However, it was unclear where the real boundary of the garden lay so Susan would have needed to check the title deeds if she was going to buy. Despite the flat's undoubted charms Susan felt, 'It's amazing to find such a large garden in Paris, but I'd prefer to have more space in the flat than the garden because I'm not going to be here enough to look after it.' Last on her list was a delightful courtyard flat on the Left Bank in the Porte Royale area which, though central, tends to be reasonably priced. For £125,000, entry was through a delightful private courtyard which, in true Parisian style, was not open to the residents. The rooms of the one-bedroomed apartment had full-size windows on both sides which meant there was plenty of light and views over the courtyard. 'This was lovely, a complete surprise. It would be wonderful to come home to after a hot day in the city.' Susan returned to the agent to ask if she could view it again, but too late – they had already accepted another offer.

Undaunted, Susan is continuing her search. Because she already has a base, she will do what she thinks is most important: 'Spend time in the one or two areas that you're drawn to. It's just as important to see them on a wet day as on a sunny one. See who's around in the area, visit the local café and shops. I think you have to put in a good bit of footwork to know you've found right place.'

> **'This was lovely, a complete surprise. It would be wonderful to come home to after a hot day in the city.'**

Check before you buy

Once you've chosen the area you think you want to live in there are a few precautionary measures to think about before you take the plunge, which will help you avoid making any serious mistakes. This introduction is intended to give you an idea of the sort of thing you should make yourself aware of. Then, with the help of a solicitor, a good estate agent, a surveyor and possibly an architect, you should avoid any mistakes.

Whatever you do, do not buy without seeing the property for yourself, however familiar you may be with the region. Unless you have spent a considerable amount of time in the area you like already, it is a good idea to rent somewhere to live for up to a year before you buy (if you are only going to be spending a limited amount of time there, this will not be as necessary). By getting acquainted with the region of your choice, you can get to know the place and all the attractions the area has to offer. There may be more than one way of getting there, so check out the alternatives to find the easiest and least expensive. If you won't have a car, see how efficient the local public transport is. Get to know the area in both the summer and the winter. It's surprising what can be revealed when the leaves have fallen from the trees, while snow can hide faults that are all too obvious in the summer sun.

Use the shops and cafés to get to know the local people and work out how well you will fit in. They will be able to give you all sorts of invaluable information and may tip you off about a house before it comes on the market. Even more valuable, they may be able to warn you off or recommend a property you have your eye on. Seek out any British expatriates living nearby. You will be able to benefit from their experience. They will know some of the pitfalls you might avoid and may also be able to recommend various professionals they have used such as estate agents, lawyers, surveyors, architects and builders. Watch how much houses in the area are selling for. This will enable you to gauge exactly what you should be offering.

If you are proposing to set up a business such as running a *gîte*, a B&B, a bar or a café, you will need to know how seasonal the business is likely to be. It is essential that you don't rely on an annual income that is unrealistic. Don't be afraid to ask advice from your neighbours who may have a similar business. Will there be room for both of you? How can you make your business different? Where are your clients going to materialise from? Be realistic about what you will be offering and whether people will want to detour to get it.

Once you've found the house you want, don't rush into buying it without some thought. Visit it at different times of the day and week to see if anything such as traffic, school noise or flight paths affect it. Even if it is not the custom in your chosen country to use a surveyor, it is advisable. An old building will not come with any guarantees and you want to be sure it's

Unless you have spent a lot of time in the area you like already, it can be a good idea to rent somewhere to live – for up to a year – before you buy

sound. Check the roof, doors and window frames. You do not want to be involved in any unforeseen costly repair work once you have bought the property. How much decoration needs to be done – be realistic here. Is any or all of the furniture included in the asking price? Make very clear exactly what you are expecting to buy and be prepared to negotiate for any extras such as garden furniture, curtains or carpets. In some places, houses are sold with all the furniture included. If you are planning to restore or build a house, you will need to establish how close it is to the mains utilities. These can be expensive connections if they are some way away. Some properties have their own natural water supply which could make things easier but you may have to budget for a septic tank or other waste-disposal system.

The most vital safety net of all is a good solicitor. Don't underestimate the value of employing someone who knows the laws of the country and the common pitfalls. They will be responsible for carrying out the local searches but be sure yourself what the exact boundaries of the property are or if any rights of way or easements run through it. Be aware that some things may hold up the buying process. For instance, in some rural areas, it may be unclear who has title to the house if it has been passed down the generations. Permission to sell must be obtained from everyone and that may take some time. In rural France, if you're buying above a certain amount of acreage, it must first be offered to the neighbouring farmers who have a limited time in which to take up the offer.

You will also need to check the planning regulations in the area. If the house you're buying is a listed building, you may be extremely limited as to what you can do with it. The local council may have strict rules about development in the region, which might prevent you from building an extra storey, an extension or a pool. You should also be sure that the previous owner received planning permission for any recent additions or extensions. If permission was overlooked, you could be forced to pull them down. Check whether the surrounding land is protected and, if not, whether there are plans for development on it. It would be devastating to move into your dream home only to discover a motorway or block of flats being constructed between you and your prized panoramic view. If you are planning to build or renovate, make sure there is planning permission before you buy, and check how long it has to run because it won't necessarily be renewed.

If you decide to buy a property off-plan in a new development, you should be very careful to check what it is you'll be buying. When you are shown the location for your home, ask what plans there are for other buildings around it. You should also check whether you will be getting exactly what you have seen in the show flat or whether there are extra upgrades that you will have to pay for. They may be restrictions on the property – quite common in America – that can dictate anything from where you can park your car to whether or not you can leave a cardigan on an outdoor chair. However, these types of property should come with a structural guarantee and have the virtue of being ready to move into right away.

Italy

Because of its climate, topographical diversity, delightful food and wines, and extraordinary cultural heritage, Italy has always been a popular destination for expatriates from northern Europe. Summers are stiflingly hot in the south, while alpine weather is enjoyed in the extreme north. Although the industrial areas around Turin, Milan and Venice are densely populated and highly sophisticated, life is simpler in the remoter parts of the country. There the pace is agreeably slow, especially in the intensely farmed countryside of Tuscany and Umbria.

Few people put more energy into their food and drink than the Italians. The most celebrated gastronomic region is around Bologna, while the pre-eminent vineyards are those of Tuscan Chianti, but every area has its own cheeses, sausages, hams, breads, sauces and wines. Pasta, ice cream and good coffee are ubiquitous. Italy's wealth of art galleries, museums, opera houses and churches – and classical ruins, reflecting 2000 years of cultural life – has made it one of the world's great tourist destinations. The most popular cities – Rome, Florence, Venice and Pisa – are so crowded in the summer months that they can seem beleaguered. But if you retreat to the cool of the hills, you will have peace restored to you.

Above *The sophisticated resort of Portofino is an expensive but irresistible option for people wanting to buy property on the Italian Riviera.*

Italy is divided into 20 regions, which are subdivided into 96 provinces. Until Unification in 1861, they were a collection of city states, duchies, kingdoms and republics. Consequently, each region has largely clung on to its own identity, customs, dialect and cuisine. However, the most striking difference lies in the division between the north and the south of this narrow peninsula. The north is characterised by its economic dynamism, whereas the area from Rome southwards, known as *il mezzogiorno*, is more economically depressed and life moves at a slower pace. The weather varies regionally too. Generally the climate is warm but the north is more temperate with winters at least as cold as Britain whereas in the south, winters are considerably milder.

In the north, Liguria, better known as the Italian Riviera, has recently begun to arouse interest with foreign homebuyers. Stretching from the Tuscan border in the east to the French border in the west, this region offers a fantastic range of locations, from magnificent beaches, which become crowded in the summer, to isolated mountain villages surrounded by olives and vines.

Genoa, birthplace of Christopher Columbus, is the region's capital. It's an eclectic city that mixes old and new but life remains centred on the warren of streets that surround its harbour, which is still Italy's most important commercial port. Recently renovated as part of the 1992 Columbus International Exposition, with the restoration of many of the dockside buildings, the port area is dominated by a giant derrick, the Grande Bigo. But the town offers more than just a rich history – it also has a wealth of restaurants, shops, theatre, opera, cinema and clubs and bars.

The Riviera itself divides in two: the Riviera di Ponente, which is west of Genoa, and the Riviera di Levante to the east. The Riviera di Ponente is the more developed, with some of the most expensive resorts in Europe, and the medieval towns of Noli and Albenga. Property prices are likely to be extremely high round here. The eastern coast is more irregular but it is worth heading for the hills where medieval villages, built in defence against Saracen invaders, spiral around hilltops. The mix of fishing villages (some of which are only accessible by boat) and mountains has captured the imagination of some of the world's greatest romantics. The gulf of La Spezia is also known as the 'Gulf of Poets', in celebration of the love that DH Lawrence and Dante, among others, had for the area. Although Ligurians have a reputation for meanness, perhaps because of their response to past hardships, their food is generous and filling. Fish is a staple of their diet. Local dishes include rich fish stews (*burrida*, *zuppa di datteri*, *zimino*) and *cappon magro*, a traditional fish and vegetable salad from Genoa. Another popular dish is *pasta alla genovese* (pasta with a basil, pine nut and garlic sauce). All are happily washed down with Cinque Terra, a local aromatic dry white wine.

Trieste is the capital of the Friuli-Venezia-Giuila region, which lies on the north-east coast of the Italian peninsula – lapped by the Adriatic and bordered by Austria and Slovenia. The region is fascinating for its geographical diversity: the alpine north offers good climbing and walking; in the south there are plains and lagoons with excellent beaches on the coast. The area is also varied ethnically, thanks to the influences of cultures that tended not to encroach on the rest of Italy: Trieste has a strong Austrian feel; Gorizia is more Eastern European; Udine seems Venetian; while Aquileia still shows evidence of its Roman origins.

While attached to Italy, the people of the region cling to their own traditions including the distinctive Friulano dialect. Ligurian cuisine tends to be simple and local dishes include gnocchi, *pasta e fagioli* (pasta and beans), meatballs, polenta, boiled meats and the famed San Daniele ham. The vineyards of Friuli-Venezia-Giuila produce first-rate wines, among them Pinot Grigio, Tocai, Grave del Friuli, and Merlot. A *resentin*, coffee in a cup washed with grappa, will guarantee a final kick to any meal.

During the 18th century, when the Austrians realised the value of the port of Trieste, they flattened its medieval centre and replaced it with the elegant neo-classical buildings that characterise the town today. After 1918, Italy took over the city but, realising it could not compete with other Italian ports, left it to decline. However, recently Trieste has begun to reinvent itself.

Above *Trieste has a long seafaring history and its position beneath the white limestone Carso overlooking the Adriatic must be one of the most alluring in Italy.*

It is worth taking a look at the other regions in the north. Lombardy offers its lakes Como, Guarda and Maggiore, the sophistication of Milan, skiing or hiking in the Alps and the fertile plains round the River Po. Veneto has attracted visitors throughout the ages. There are many wonderful attractions but the most famous is the awe-inspiring, water-bound city of Venice. Emilia Romagna not only prides itself on having the best cuisine in Italy, but also boasts a charming capital, Bologna, busy Adriatic resorts and magnificent hiking in the Appenines. In all these areas property is pricey but ideal town and country hideaways can be found.

Central Italy has always been the most popular area with British expatriates. Tuscany, or 'Chianti-shire' as it has come to be known, is the favourite spot, with Umbria and Marche coming close behind. Tuscany, with its temperate climate, distinctive rolling landscape of olive groves, vineyards and small hill towns, also offers major attractions such as Florence, Pisa, Siena and Lucca. The combination of an agreeable climate, ravishing scenery and beautiful historic towns has made it a magnet for holidaymakers and house-hunters.

The principal city of Florence is overwhelming in its art, culture and history. Built on the banks of the Arno, the city is a living museum. It contains a multitude of art galleries, museums, palaces and churches, including the Uffizi, the Bargello, the Pitti Palace and the familiar landmark of Brunelleschi's Duomo, which rises above the city. Despite the noisy traffic, Florence remains one of the most captivating cities in the world – you can indulge a passion for Renaissance art and architecture, sit in open-air cafés watching the world go by, or wander the narrow streets. Crossing the river via the celebrated Ponte Vecchio – crowded with tiny shops – will take you towards the welcome serenity of the Boboli gardens.

Property lawyer, Rosie Wilson, and her daughter, Zoe, came to look at the possibilities offered by the region and concentrated on the area around Lucca, a quiet medieval

Facts

Capital Rome
Population 57,634,000
Land area 301,230 sq km
Currency 1 Italian lira (Lit) =
    100 centesimi
    Euro from 2002
Electricity 220v
Time zone GMT + 1 hour
Religion Predominately Roman
    Catholic
Language Italian
Government Republic

Above *Villages in the rolling Tuscan countryside continue to be a favourite with British buyers in Italy.*

town within sturdy city walls, set in Tuscany's richest agricultural region. 'I love the Italian culture. I'm passionate about opera and particularly about Puccini who came from here. I'm looking for something with some land within the environs of Lucca, with space for a pool and a grand piano.' Tuscany is scattered with smaller medieval towns such as San Gimignano, Cortona or Montepulciano, all of them surrounded by vineyards, wheat fields and pine forests. The scenery is simply breathtaking. Property in Tuscany does not come cheap anymore. Many of the classic stone farmhouses have been restored and come on to the market highly priced. Even if you are lucky enough to find one in need of restoration, don't expect to pick up a bargain.

Simplicity is the watchword for Tuscan cuisine, grilled steak (*bistecca alla fiorentina*) being a good example. Otherwise, grilled meats of any kind find their way on to the menu as well as beans, local cheeses and sweet biscuits (*cantucci*) which are dipped into *vin santo*.

Prices tend to be more reasonable in neighbouring Umbria. Known as 'the green heart of Italy', its lush countryside and woodlands run with rivers and streams. It has the benefit of having fewer tourists and foreign property owners than Tuscany, but the situation is changing fast. Umbria has two principal towns: Perugia and Assisi. Assisi, birthplace of Italy's patron saint, St Francis, was badly damaged in the 1997 earthquake. It is home to the Basilico de San Francisco, the 14th-century castle Rocca Maggiore, the Duomo and the unscathed Templo di Minerva. The medieval centre of Perugia is surrounded by modern suburbs, often industrial, but it has maintained a strong artistic and cultural tradition. Every summer the city buzzes with the international festival, Umbria Jazz. The University for Foreigners, set up by Mussolini in 1925, attracts students from all over the world who give the city a surprising cosmopolitan flavour. It also runs short courses in Italian, which might be useful for new homeowners still struggling to master the language.

Umbria also has various enchanting smaller towns, particularly in the north. Spoleto is noted for its Festival of the Two Worlds, an international celebration of drama, music and dance; Todi and Gubbio are heralded as two of Italy's best preserved medieval towns. Generally, the local architecture is similar to that of Tuscany. The people enjoy good wholesome cooking and the special ingredient in Umbrian cuisine is the black truffle (*tartufo nero*), which is celebrated in summer festivals throughout the region. Norcia is famous for its pork sausages and lentils. Other specialities include spit-roasted meat, especially suckling pig (*porchetta*), wild asparagus and mushrooms.

Marche occupies a narrow strip between the Appennines and the Adriatic – some would say it is Italy's best-kept secret. There are hundreds of places to explore but the best known are: Urbino, with its spectacular Renaissance palace and home of the painter, Raphael; Macerata, as fetching as any Tuscan or Umbrian hill town but minus the crowds; Ascoli Piceno, which allegedly owes its existence to a woodpecker that led a group of nomadic shepherds to settle there; Jesi, known as 'the little Milan of the north' and celebrated for its Renaissance and Baroque palaces, most notably the Palazzo Pianetti; the pilgrimage site of Loreto; and the small spa town of Sarnano.

The pace is slow here, the people friendly and the scenery is magnificent, with wonderful walking possibilities in the Monti Sibellini. There are elegant *palazzi* as well as attractive white stone farmhouses and cottages, frequently in need of renovation and sometimes hard to access. Fish stew (*brodetto di pesci*), using different fish in tomato sauce, is served all along the coast. Inland, the traditional first course is *vincigrassi*, a rich lasagne which is best washed down with local wines such as Rosso del Conero or Verdicchio dei Castelli di Jesi.

The attractions of Rome are legion, despite the crowds and pollution that characterise almost any capital city nowadays. It is vibrant, cosmopolitan and attracts a huge number of foreign residents, ensuring a good number of international schools and expatriate organisations. Built on seven hills, Rome was the capital of Christianity and seat of the Papal States before it was chosen as Italy's capital in 1870 due to its strategic position between the northern and southern regions. The Roman remains of the Colosseum, the Forum, the Pantheon and the Palatine Hill rub shoulders with Baroque fountains, Romanesque churches, Renaissance palaces and buildings dating from the Unification.

The *centro storico*, or historical centre, largely falls within the loop of the river Tiber and is the area where the majority of tourists go. Narrow streets flanked by tall buildings open on to wide open piazzas with splashing fountains where cafés ply a busy trade throughout the day and evening. But there are other quarters of Rome which are as fascinating with their own distinct character: the wealthy neighbourhood of Parioli, north of the Villa Borghese; the bustling Bohemian Trastevere; the maze of the Jewish Ghetto; the EUR (Esposizione Universale di Roma), a satellite city built by Mussolini; and the fashionable Testaccio with its clubs and trattorias. Rome is also unique because another city exists within it – the walled Vatican City. Established as an independent sovereign city in 1929, it has its own police force, postal system, radio station and newspaper. Its walls open on to St Peter's Basilica and Square where thousands of pilgrims come every year.

North of the city the landscape is green and wooded with lakes Bracciano, Vico and Bolsena providing welcome relief in the heat of the summer. The shores of these

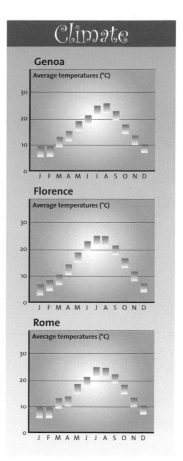

Climate

Genoa
Average temperatures (°C)

Florence
Average temperatures (°C)

Rome
Average temperatures (°C)

Left *The real charm of Marche lies away from the crowded beaches in small medieval hill towns such as Urbino.*

Above Trulli, circular stone houses with conical roofs, are unique to Puglia and can be found in and around Alberobello.

lakes are far more attractive than the nearest coastline. The region is known for its Etruscan archaeological sites, particularly at Tarquinia and Cerveteri, and for the splendid villas that were built by Romans as their country houses. Further south, the 13 castle towns, *Castelli Romani*, including Frascati, Rocca di Papa and Grottaferrata, are now popular with Romans seeking second homes. The Pope has his summer retreat at Castel Gandolfo. The coast offers various resort possibilities, which are definitely more pleasant south of the capital. Resorts include Terracina, Sperlonga, Gaeta, Formia and the island of Ponza, which is easily accessible from the mainland by ferry and boasts one of the prettiest pastel-coloured towns on the seaboard.

Property prices tend to be relatively high in the countryside around Rome because the Romans often commute from out of town. This has had the benefit of ensuring communications are excellent regionally, nationally and internationally. Cuisine in the region is unpretentious. Appearing on the menu are pasta dishes with thick sauces, offal, and dishes such as *saltimbocca all romana* (veal with ham and sage) or *trippa alla romana* (tripe in tomato and vegetable sauce). Of the vegetables, *carciofi alla romana* (artichokes) is a particular speciality. As for wine, Frascati, Velletri and Olivano are a few that originate in this productive region.

Further south is the region of Puglia, the heel of the boot, surrounded by the Adriatic and Ionian seas. It is Italy's major olive- and wheat-growing area, with a rich history still evident in its Baroque and Romanesque architecture, a number of impressive castles that date back to Frederick II and the atmospheric old quarters of various towns.

Puglia's different landscapes range from the desert-like Salentine peninsula – the tip of the heel – to the mountainous central area of Le Murge, and the forests and beaches of the Gargano peninsula – the spur. Pilgrims have been visiting Monte Sant' Angelo for centuries to celebrate the alleged appearance of the archangel Michael; today sun worshippers flock there to enjoy the beaches and lagoons of the north side and the rocky coves of the south. Vieste is the main town of the region, a lively resort that is a great base for the Trémiti Islands or the beaches, caves and grottoes of the coast. Inland, the Foresta Umbra draws people with its wildlife and numerous marked trails for walkers. Gastronomic specialities of the region include *pancotto* (bread soup), *coniglio ai capperi* (rabbit cooked with capers), *ostriche* (fresh oysters baked with bread crumbs), and *orrechiette alla barese* (pasta with broccoli, garlic, anchovy and hot peppers), all of which might be happily accompanied by a glass of the local Sansevero, Santo Stefano or Aleatico di Puglia.

The rest of southern Italy is composed of the regions of Campania, Basilicata and Calabria. Because of the earthquake risk, the heat, and the threat of the Mafia, the British have tended to stay in central and northern Italy. But there are places of extreme beauty and historical interest in southern Italy, too – it's just a question of taking time to explore and deciding what will best meet your needs. If you choose the region that appeals to you most, there's every chance you will find your own piece of paradise.

How to get there

Air
British Airways and Alitalia fly from Heathrow and Gatwick to Bologna, Milan, Naples, Pisa, Rome, Turin and Venice; from Manchester to Milan and Rome. Various charter companies also operate.
Flight time: 2½–4 hours

How to buy property in...
Italy

Italian law goes a long way to protect foreign property buyers but, as with every country, it is advisable to seek your own independent legal advice before you sign anything or transfer money. This basic guide will give you an idea of the process.

For your own protection, it's advisable to use an estate agent registered with the local Chamber of Commerce. Having found the property but before signing the preliminary contract (*compromesso*), you will need to conduct a survey, local searches and check that the property confirms with local planning and building regulations. This work is usually carried out by a surveyor (*geometra*) who will provide a written report. The *compromesso* can be drawn up by the vendor, the estate agent, a notary (*notaio*) or a lawyer. This document should include the terms of the sale: details of the property, the seller and buyer, the price, how the purchase will be financed and the completion date. It should also give details of any other conditions that have to be completed before the sale, for example whether the buyer is able to obtain a mortgage or planning permission, or the discovery of local plans to build something that will affect the property.

At this stage a deposit (*caparra* or *deposito*) of anything between 10 and 30 per cent is payable to the seller. Make sure you are absolutely clear about the terms of the deposit and under what circumstances it might be returned.

It is possible to register the *compromesso* with the local Registration Tax office. This has the advantage of preventing another prospective buyer getting involved because he will be informed of the existence of your *compromesso* when he conducts his local searches. You will need to make sure that the property is in the condition you saw it when you made your original offer and that it includes everything you agreed to buy. Make a visit with your lawyer to check. Consult your lawyer or estate agent about the declaration of value, which is normally 10 to 20 per cent lower than the purchase price.

This is an Italian ploy to avoid capital gains tax and provides the figure that will determine the rate of Italian Registration Tax (*imposta di registro*) – 4 per cent for a new property, 11 per cent for other houses and apartments, and 17 per cent for agricultural land.

By the time you are ready to complete, you must have fulfilled all the conditions in the contract and obtained an Italian tax code number (*codice fiscale*). Completion must take place in front of a *notaio* appointed and paid for by the buyer. He is an independent representative of the government, who has the authority to transfer legal title to properties. If the buyer is not fluent in Italian, then an officially accredited interpreter must be present or the buyer must give power of attorney to his lawyer or estate agent. Before signing, the balance of the money due to the seller, the *notaio*'s fees and any relevant taxes are presented, preferably in the form of a banker's draft. After signature, the property is yours.

All that remains is for the *notaio* to register the new title deed at the Land Registry. The buyer should collect a copy of the purchase deed from the *notaio*'s office a couple of weeks later. The *notaio* will provide the buyer with a form with which to notify the local police of the purchase. Now you need to inform the mains suppliers of the change in ownership of the property and then you can sit back and enjoy it. Estate agents' fees, which are usually about 4 per cent, are often split 50/50 between the buyer and seller.

House-hunter

Guy Dunhill

Antiques dealer Guy Dunhill, studied furniture restoration in Florence and came to know the area well. 'That was about 10 years ago and I've been desperate to come back ever since. I loved the food, the architecture, the people and the culture.' Guy is working to a budget of £150,000 plus a further £100,000 for renovation. He hopes to find the ideal property to convert into a five-bedroomed house with a pool and tennis court, and outbuildings that could be used as *gîtes* in the summer months. 'My plan is to export antiques to Italy and take back modern Italian designerware, maybe ceramics or bathroom products, to sell in England.'

The first property he saw was in Casteluccio on the upper Arno. The house was typical of the region with four rooms, a kitchen, three outbuildings, a stable and 1.7 acres of land that led down to the river and included a vineyard, fig trees and an outhouse by the river. It was on the market for £141,000. Guy could see the potential of the buildings and appreciated the possibility of buying some extra adjoining land, but felt it was too close to the neighbours. Moving further south to the picturesque town of Cortona – surrounded by olive groves and rich valley farmland – he looked at a 200-year-old farmhouse. Six large rooms and a kitchen plus various outbuildings and pigsties surrounded by three acres of land were offered for £78,250. The amount of work needed to restore them was reflected in the price but Guy was excited by the idea of the project, aware that he would have to work within the strict regional planning regulations.

Left *Although this property in Marche fulfilled all of Guy's requirements, it was not the house of his dreams.*

Before making up his mind he was shown a mountain retreat in Marche. A defunct tobacco farm with unusual outbuildings, including a drying house, sat in seven acres of land and was being sold for £110,000. It was another property with enormous potential to create the sort of home that Guy was looking for, but in the end he decided the symmetric design of the large farmhouse was too rigid. So it was on to the outskirts of Arezzo, where two dilapidated houses hidden in pine forests overlooking the town could provide a comfortable six- to seven-bedroomed house among its own 148 acres of land. The sensational 360° views clinched Guy's decision and he made an offer. 'I returned to England and asked for the paperwork to be sent to my Italian lawyer here. I chased it but it never materialised, then when I phoned the architect who was handling the sale, I was told if I wanted it, I would have to pay considerably more.'

Guy decided to look for something else, concentrating his searches within a half hour's drive from Arezzo because of its reputation as a centre for antiques. 'There's plenty of property to look at here. The Italian inheritance laws mean that small farmers can amass as many as four or five house over the generations. Some farmers would rather see them fall to pieces, others prefer to sell. Many of them retain property as investments or to pass on to their children when they marry.' House-hunting in Italy is dangerously time-consuming. It can take a day to see only a couple of properties. 'Unless you speak fluent Italian, you can only deal with about 10 per cent of the agents here. I've found this so often, I've considered setting up my own agency to assist in the buying and restoration of these types of property.'

At last, after more concentrated searching, Guy has set his heart on a house priced at £130,000 he's found through an Italian property magazine. 'There are two small buildings on either side of it which I'd like to negotiate for too. It also has the virtue of being partially restored with a new roof, new windows and drainage.' Guy and his fiancée, Kerry, are planning a summer wedding in Arezzo and he has great hopes that this will be their first dream home.

'I studied furniture restoration in Florence and I've been desperate to come back ever since. I loved the food, the architecture, the people and the culture.'

Relocation

Residence and Work Permits – Property Restrictions – Benefits and Pensions – Healthcare

Do not assume that you can move to a particular country for any length of time until you have checked out its residency requirements. Some countries are extremely strict about how long foreigners can stay. Similarly, if you plan to work abroad, investigate whether or not it will be legally permissible. If you are relocated by a company you already work for, they will take care of the necessary formalities for you. However, if you intend to find employment yourself or set up your own business, make sure that you will be eligible for the appropriate permits. Breaches of these regulations are taken extremely seriously, so research the situation thoroughly. Legislation can change, so it is always advisable to contact the relevant embassy or consulate for up-to-date advice.

Countries in the EU allow any EU nationals to work and live there although residency permits are not automatically granted and would-be residents may have to prove a certain minimum level of income, particularly if they are pensioners. Most countries admit visitors for a 90-day period, though they may insist on registration with the local police, embassy or consulate, after which some form of temporary residence permit is needed. The fee for a permit and the length of time it covers varies from country to country. After a certain number of years, a permanent residency can be applied for which may need to be regularly renewed. Moving to some EU countries (such as Italy, Spain or Portugal) will entail applying for a fiscal number (or its equivalent), without which financial transactions are impossible.

Non-resident foreigners can buy property in America but have a limited amount of time they can spend there. Entry to the country is strictly controlled, although visa waivers entitle holders to a 90-day stay. In reality, most non-resident visitors can remain in the country for a maximum of six months in any one year. Foreigners cannot retire to Florida or move to work there without a permanent residence permit or 'green card' – neither owning a property nor having enough money to support yourself is enough to get one. It is important to investigate whether or not you are eligible before you make any plans and, with many different types of visas on offer, specialist attorney or consultancy advice is essential as successful applications are extremely limited.

Some countries restrict foreigners from buying more than a specified area of land or more than one property at a time (Cyprus), or may specify areas where they are not allowed to buy at all (Turkey). Make sure you are not about to flout any such regulations before you sign any contract or hand over any money.

If you are planning to rent the property for part of each year, you will need to make yourself aware of any rental restrictions attached to your property. These may adversely affect your planned rental income, and the length of time you will be able to rent it or spend there yourself. In countries outside the EU, it is advisable to check whether there are additional or unusual restrictions on purchasing property. For instance, in the Caribbean, some islands require a prospective foreign buyer to have an Alien Landholder's Certificate; in Bulgaria, you can currently only acquire the land a property sits on if you establish a company there. In those countries where you cannot rent out a property as an individual, investigate the possibilities of letting through a management company.

If you are planning to retire to a country within the EU or to America, you will be entitled to your state pension and will receive the annual increases and Christmas bonus – although you will forfeit the winter fuel allowance. If you are moving elsewhere, you should check whether the country has a reciprocal agreement with the UK. If it does not, then your pension will be frozen at the time of your departure. Your pension can be paid by credit transfer to some countries by standing order payable to your bank or to you directly. If you retain a bank or building society account in the UK, it can be paid directly into that. If you are in receipt of any other benefits, you should check with the DSS (08459 154 811) whether or not you will be able to export them abroad.

When moving to another country, you may be concerned by the level of healthcare that will be available to you there. Most EU countries offer residents some form of healthcare equivalent to our NHS (or better) but the detail of what is covered, and the terms on which it is available vary widely. Check. You may want to top up your insurance cover. Few other countries have this, and you may find that in order to get the standard of care you require it is necessary to take out adequate health insurance. In some countries this is a prerequisite of residency. Investigate the different policies available and make sure you read the small print to know exactly what is covered and for how long.

A further consideration when moving abroad is taxation. You need to be confident that you are aware of all the taxes connected with owning a property for which you will be liable. These may include property tax, land tax, wealth tax, capital gains tax, inheritance tax and tax on the rental of the property. If you are becoming a permanent resident of a country, and especially if you plan to work, you will need to familiarise yourself with income tax rates and any other taxes you will be liable to pay. In most countries if you stay there for longer than 183 days, you become liable for income tax. In many instances, however, it may prove an opportunity to reduce your tax liability if you are moving to a tax haven or to a country with low taxation. Some countries do offer tax incentives to encourage other nationalities to take residency; these benefits are often directed at people of retirement age. The timing of your move can also affect your tax position. Take sound professional financial advice to make sure you are fully aware of the implications of your move on your finances.

Some countries are extremely strict about how long foreigners can stay. Similarly, if you plan to work abroad, investigate whether or not it will be legally permissible.

Greece

reece has a wide variety of landscapes to choose from, ranging from the mountains of eastern Roumeli and the valleys and gorges of the northern Peloponnese, to the barren Mani peninsula or the many islands speckling the Aegean, Mediterranean and Ionian Seas. With a history of thousands of years of civilisation, Greece combines a huge range of fascinating influences – Hellenic, Roman, Byzantine, Ottoman and Italian. There are historic sites all over the country that testify to its rich and diverse past. Monasteries lie hidden on inland hillsides or perched on clifftops overlooking the sea, and shrines and chapels ornament the landscape.

Whitewashed villages cluster in the heat of the summer sun; their narrow streets provide welcome shade, and trails of bougainvillea and geraniums tumble brightly over the walls. Robed and bearded priests sit with village elders in the sleepy squares while skinny cats and dogs scrounge for food. Fishermen land their catch close to cafés and tavernas lining the quayside. The smells of pine, herbs and citrus blossom are carried along with the sound of bazouki music on the offshore breezes. A simple, and sometimes primitive, way of life, perhaps, but for many prospective buyers rural and coastal Greece will provide a fine and hospitable refuge from the pressures of modern life.

Facts

Capital Athens
Population 10,602,000
Land area 131,940 sq km
Currency 1 drachma (Dr) =
    100 lepta
    Euro from 2002
Electricity 220v
Time zone GMT + 2 hours
Religion Orthodox
Language Greek
Government Parliamentary
    republic

Greece has not attracted a huge number of foreign property buyers until recently, so generally there is a lot of land and property available at relatively reasonable prices, both in mainland Greece and on its many islands. It is possible to buy land on which to build, but it should be noted that in various areas there are strict planning controls over development.

Away from the major towns and resort areas, the countryside and fishing villages are unspoilt and life follows time-honoured patterns. Greek cuisine is simple and varies from region to region, depending on the local produce available. In restaurants the food is generally cooked in the morning and served throughout the day as it cools down. Favourites are the oven-baked dishes such as *moussaká* (aubergine and minced lamb), *pastítsio* (maccaroni) or rich stews. In addition, there is plenty of grilled meat and fish preceded by *mezédhes* – titbits of octopus, squid, *taramasalata*, *houmous* or *tzadziki*.

There are many places to consider when searching for a home in Greece. If you are looking for the simple island life, then ideally you should visit several before you make a final choice. Similarly, the mainland offers an astonishing array of possibilities. Among the many areas of interest in the northern region of Macedonia, the prefecture of Pieria, west of Thessaloníki, must have the biggest draw. Mount Olympus, home of the gods and the most dramatic mountain in Greece, rises impressively from the Thermaic Gulf. Its sides are heavily forested and carpeted with wild flowers in spring, and the mountain offers testing conditions for hikers. At the foot of Mount Olympus is the old summer resort of Litóhoro, which has splendid mountain views and is one of the best places from which to start an ascent. The shores of Pieria extend 70 kilometres from Platámonas to Aeginia – long sandy stretches interrupted by pine forests and olive groves. The coastal town of Katerini, with its colourful main square and fishing port, is the principal town of the region. The climate is extreme, with baking hot summers and winters cold enough to allow skiing on Mount Olympus. The area is popular with Greek

Below Galaxhídi is an unspoiled port of great character with a picture-postcard harbour partly lined with restored 19th-century houses.

A Place in the Sun

holidaymakers but has potential for British homebuyers, as Jenny Akehurst and her partner, Chris Jones, found out. 'I worked in Piraeus for four months and felt then that the Greek people are my spiritual counterpart. They are more inclusive than the British and seem to love me being an aging hippie. This part of Greece feels like unexplored territory and we feel like pioneers getting here before the tourists. The area is stunning, with the sea and mountains being so close together. The weather is milder than further south, so it's much greener.'

To the south is the rich agricultural land of Thessaly, which is surrounded by mountain ranges and includes the busy towns of Lárisa, Vólos and Kalambáka. The Pilion peninsula is cloaked in forests and fruit orchards and contains some of the prettiest inland and coastal villages in Greece. The peninsula is cooler in summer than much of the mainland, which makes it a popular place with Greek holidaymakers, though it is largely undiscovered by the British. The northern shore of the Gulf of Corinth is popular with Athenians seeking relief from the city heat. Reputed to have the most agreeable climate in Greece, it has mild winters and cool summers.

The two main resort towns are Návpaktos and Galaxhídi. Návpaktos is the livelier of the two; its old quarter is embraced by the walls of the large Venetian castle that rise on the hill behind the new town. There are plenty of busy tavernas and restaurants lining the harbour and beachfronts. Galaxhídi's beach is minimal but the town is ideal for a hideaway within easy reach of many of the attractions of mainland Greece. Nearby is Aráhova, popular with the smart, Athenian set. It is relatively expensive but is one of the most seductive towns in the area. It has narrow streets that wind up the hillside, and traditional houses and shops that sell the local wine, sheepskin rugs and honey. Otherwise there are villages such as Pendápolis and Amfissa tucked into the foothills where you will be guaranteed a life away from it all.

Across the canal the Peloponnese peninsula is divided into seven prefectures. Between them they represent everything that is Greek. There are superb archaeological sites at Epidavros, Mycenae and Pilos, perfect undiscovered beaches on the west coast, and dramatic interior landscapes. Olives, figs, citrus fruits, grapes and honey are some of the region's most prized products. Patras is the largest city in the prefecture of Achaia, with a charming old town of neo-classical buildings, pleasant parks and squares overlooked by its castle. The coastline is pitted with coves, forests and picture-perfect villages: Akrata, Platanos, Trapeza and Diakofto. Behind rise the foothills of the Helmos mountains where the air is cooler, and plane and walnut trees shade the roads on the way to hamlets such as Zahlorou, Kalanitsa, Mihas and Vlassia. Best of all is Kalavrita, a peaceful haven in summer, ski resort in winter.

In the south-west, the Messinian coast has plenty to offer the British abroad. The capital of the region, Kalamata, spreads beneath a 13th-century castle and hugs the curved shore of the Ionian sea. This is a town that has plenty to offer in terms of culture, with concerts and plays gracing the amphitheatre of the castle every summer. Sleepy in the heat of the day, the town wakes up at night. The waterfront becomes alive with tavernas plying roast suckling pig, chicken, olives, cheese and, naturally, the ubiquitous *raki* and *retsina*. To the west, beaches stretch all the way past Petalídhi to Koroni, where tiled pastel houses in narrow, scrambling streets provide some great possibilities for expatriate home owners.

Inland, the mountainous landscape is carved with deep gorges forested with pine trees. Tucked away here are villages, ruins of early settlements, medieval castles and Byzantine churches. Travelling into the Mani is to enter another world. Crags plunge down to the sea and hidden pebbly coves. Along the coast road are pleasant small resorts such as Kárdamili and Stoupa, and small fishing villages protected in natural harbours. Further south things get quieter, the landscape becomes more hostile and the hillside villages languish almost empty.

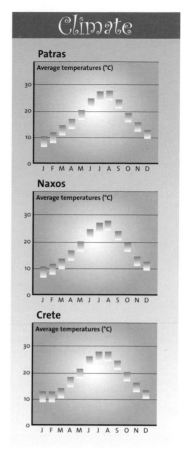

Climate

Patras

Average temperatures (°C)

Naxos

Average temperatures (°C)

Crete

Average temperatures (°C)

The capital city, Athens, is noisy and dirty yet still retains some of its seductive charms. The Athenians are friendly and gregarious and you will find suburbs where elegant mansions and attractive, newly built houses and gardens are predominant. Unless you are transferring on business, it's unlikely that you'll want to set up home here but it may still be your jumping-off point for exploring other parts of Greece. The international airport is just outside the city and Píraeus is its busy port. From here, ferries set off to all the islands, although many of them are now served by their own airports.

The Sporades

The Sporades, off the northern mainland, are mountainous and wooded with splendid beaches and clean sea. They include Évvia, second largest island in Greece to Crete, Skíathos, Skópelos, Alónnisos and Skíros.

Skíathos and Skópelos are among the most commercialised Greek islands with the result that

Above Restoring houses in traditional style ensures the island of Alónnissos keeps its Sporadan character unspoiled.

property tends to be quite expensive. The capital town of Skíathos is very developed and is the centre for all ferry traffic to the island. The island also has its own airport. The road south from Skíathos winds round the Kalamáki peninsula. The peninsula offers good beaches and watersports as far as Koukounariés, which claims to have the best beach in Greece. In the north, the beaches are less protected from the *meltémi*, the prevailing summer wind. Inland, pine forests and olive groves hide farmhouses, deserted monasteries, churches and the abandoned village of Kástro in the north. In the south, there are enchanting villages to be found basking in the sun.

Skópelos has been occupied by various nations over the centuries. It is more cultivated than Skiáthos, boasting excellent fruit orchards as well as pine forests and golden beaches. The slate-roofed houses of Skópelos town slope down from the whitewashed Venetian Kástro to the large bay below, where activity centres on the busy quayside. Its charm is rivalled by that of Glossa, in the north-west, situated high above the small port of Loutráki. Here, reminders of Venetian occupation are seen in the architecture, many of the houses whitewashed with brightly painted doors and shutters. The main resorts are south of Skópelos town, from the beachless Agnóndas, to the pebbles of Miliá and the resorts of Pánormos and Elios. The main features of the interior of the island are plum orchards and *kalívias*, fine stone farmhouses. Fay Corbett fell under the island's spell, although for personal reasons she eventually opted to look for property closer to home. 'I came here with an open mind and discovered that I love Greek people and this island. There's a lot of climbing and the traditional houses seem to have little outdoor space, but it is so beautiful.'

The Cyclades

This disparate group of 56 islands meets every homeowner's Greek fantasy. The islands' name comes from the Greek *kyklo* (circle) because they circled the sacred isle of Delos, now an important archaeological site. They include the spectacular, volcanic Santorini; the pigrimage centre of Tinos; Mykonos and Ios with their legendary nightlife; and Syrós, the commercial and regional centre. The two islands of Naxos and Paros are where retired company director, Jeff Simmons, and his wife, Mary, decided to search out a holiday home. 'They offer a completely contrasting style and pace of life to most other European holiday destinations. The numerous ferries also offer many alternative island excursions. The almost crime-free and leisurely way of life and the many inexpensive and friendly restaurants serving fresh, healthy food make them our first choice.'

Naxos is the largest island in the group and boasts its own airport. Its occupation by the Venetians for three centuries from 1207 has left fortified towers (*pyrgoi*) and mansions throughout the interior. The highlights of Naxos town include the giant stone gateway from the unfinished Temple of Apollo and the fortified Venetian Kástro. The island's many visitors tend to stick to the tried and tested beaches south of the main town. Inland, the countryside is a dramatic combination of craggy mountains, vineyards, orchards, citrus and olive groves, and delightful villages where the real island life can be found. The Traía valley features picturesque villages such as Halkí, Moní, Filotí and Cretan-influenced Apíranthos, and provides opportunities for good hiking. In the north, there's the emery-miners' town of Komíaki, where the local lemon liqueur *kitrón* originated; on the coast is the fishing village of Apóllon, which is situated beneath the ancient marble quarry where an unfinished statue of Apollo still lies.

Famous for the white marble that ensured its prosperity through the ages, Paros is now a green, scented island that relies on the tourist trade for its wealth. The main town of Parikiá still has traces of its Venetian and Byzantine past, particularly in the Ekatontapylianí, the oldest church in Greece. There's a busy waterfront with a delightful old town behind, complete with winding white alleys and medieval arches. The two other major towns are Náousa, a colourful, cosmopolitan fishing harbour, and Léfkes, an unspoiled mountain village with a maze of medieval streets and squares. Paros has everything, including monasteries, busy fishing villages, great beaches and an exciting night life. Its satellite island of Antíparos has a stylish main town, fine beaches and the awe-inspiring Cave of Antíparos – a calm, alternative sun filled spot.

Crete

Crete is the largest and most significant southern point in Europe. A barrier of mountain ranges divides the north of the island from the south, making access between them difficult. The main towns are spread along the north coast, while the rugged south coast is indented with coves and is less crowded. The climate is mild in the winter but can be very hot in the summer. Cretan people are friendly and generous,

Left *Réthymnon is a charming beachfront town with a palm-lined promenade busy with cafes and tavernas.*

particularly in the rural areas where life goes on much the same as it has for centuries.

The capital of Iráklion is the main town of the island, situated close to the airport and with a large ferry port. The coastal strip east of the city is very developed, though it's possible to escape the crowds further east or south. The principal resort of eastern Crete is the renowned but picturesque Aghios Nikalaos, but further along the peninsula life gets quieter. Inland, the agricultural plain of Lásithiou is famed for its windmills and surrounded by pleasant Cretan villages.

Eastern Crete may have the monopoly on culture but western Crete cannot be bettered in terms of beaches. From Iráklion to Réthymnon, the sea slaps against steep cliffs, but then the coastline changes into long stretches of sun-kissed sand, the best extending from Chaniá to Máleme. Chánia's delightful harbour is lined with pastel-coloured houses with orange-tiled roofs and there is evidence of Venetian occupation everywhere. The peaks of the Lefká Óri provide a dramatic backdrop and offer good walking, climbing and even skiing. Crete is popular with foreign homebuyers, as it has its own airport, but property does tend to be more expensive than on the other islands.

The Ionian Islands

The Ionian islands are to the west of mainland Greece and include Corfu, Paxos, Lefkádha, Kefalloniá, Zákinthos, Itháki and Kíthira. Unlike most of the Aegean islands, they have lush vegetation thanks to reliable winter rain.

Although a popular package-holiday destination, Corfu still retains parts where it's possible to escape the hordes and find traditional hill villages and secluded coves. Highlights of the island include Corfu town, which contains a wealth of European influences; Korisíon Lagoon, a haven for wildlife; and the Achílleion Palace, built for Elizabeth of Austria. With beautiful beaches and plenty to explore, the island has long been popular with British people seeking their dream home.

Kefalloniá is the largest island of the group and is currently enjoying a boost to its reputation as the setting to Louis de Bernière's celebrated novel, *Captain Corelli's Mandolin*. The main town of Argostóli was flattened in the 1953 earthquake but it has since been rebuilt into a thriving town. The principal port is Samí. The liveliest resorts are on the south coast, from Lassí all the way round to Póros. Jack and Susan Bedoyan came here searching for a place to retire in the sun. 'Some years ago we had a holiday in Lefkas, one of the other Ionian islands, and we both liked the area very much. We also heard that Kefallonia was a beautiful island but I knew this from stories my mother used to tell me from the time she spent there as a young refugee from Turkey. Of course, there are all the other usual reasons: the sun, the blue sea, the food, the music, the aroma of wild herbs growing all over the island, the laid-back way the people live in these islands and the fantastic sailing.'

Above Kefalloniá is perennially popular with homebuyers because of its unspoiled towns, quiet inland villages, excellent beaches and breathtaking scenery.

How to get there

Air
Olympic Airways and British Airways fly from Heathrow to Athens and Thessaloniki. Virgin Airlines fly to Athens. Local flights can be booked with Olympic Airways or Cronus Airlines. Charter flights are available to the mainland and islands from major tour operators.
Flight time: 3 hours

A Place in the Sun

How to buy property in...
Greece

It is essential to employ a lawyer to handle your affairs when buying a property in Greece. There are English-speaking local lawyers or you may prefer to use one based in the UK.

Once your offer has been accepted, a preliminary contract is drawn up in front of the notary. This should contain the names and addresses of the buyer and seller, the description of the property, the price, the means of payment and any other conditions deemed necessary by either party. These may relate to ensuring that you obtain vacant possession, checking that the property is unencumbered by debt, confirming the boundaries or making sure that planning permission has not been granted for a 16-storey apartment block right in front of the property. In Greece, it is possible for more than one person to have title to the property. Each person must agree to the sale. If that's the case, it's wise to find out how long it will take to obtain a clear title deed before you sign the contract. On signature, a deposit is paid, generally 10 per cent of the purchase price though it may be higher. If the purchaser backs out, he will forfeit the deposit. If the seller backs out, the deposit will be returned to the buyer and an equal sum be paid to him by the vendor as an indemnity.

The purchaser's lawyer is responsible for checking that the title to the property to ensure it is clear and carrying out the necessary searches with the local Land Registry. If the property is new or has been extensively restored, he will check planning permission was granted to the builder/developer or previous owner. He will work within the local regulations to ascertain that the 'fixed value' or 'officially estimated price' of the property is usually less than the purchase price. This is important because it determines the purchase tax due plus the notary and lawyer's fees. He will also ensure that the conditional clauses in the contract are fulfilled. Before registering the title deed, make sure you understand the implications as far as inheritance law and tax are concerned. Seek advice from your lawyer.

When the papers are in order, the final contract is signed before the local notary in the presence of the buyer's and seller's lawyers and, if you don't speak Greek, a translator. At this stage the balance of the purchase price is paid along with the purchase tax (between 9 and 13 per cent of the fixed value), the notary's fee (2 per cent of the fixed value) and the lawyer's fee (between 1.5 and 2 per cent of the fixed value). Greece does not allow 100 per cent foreign title ownership, but allows for 'nominees' to hold 1 per cent title to complete the sale.

There is an annual property tax, so you will need a tax number from the local Greek tax office. The tax depends on the location of the property and other variables, and is based on tables drawn up by the Greek Ministry of Finance.

Useful Addresses

Greek Embassy and Consulate General
1a Holland Park
London W11 3TP
Tel: 020 7221 6467

National Tourist Office of Greece
4 Conduit Street
London W1R 0DJ
Tel: 020 7734 5997

House-hunter

'01 05 22

Above Linda's place in the sun was built only two years ago in traditional Cretan style.

Linda Norris

Running her tea-room in Wiltshire, Linda Norris would daydream of living in Crete. After five years holidaying there, she had fallen in love with the 'beautiful island, the hospitable friendly people and the glorious climate.' Finally she decided to take the plunge. 'It's a big step but my heart's there. Each time I've visited I've made new friends and I'm only a three-and-a-half hour flight from Bristol so friends and family can reach me easily. I'll enjoy a completely different way of life.'

The first house she looked at was in Kalyves on the Vámos peninsula. Now a popular resort, it has retained a small-town atmosphere with its narrow streets and pavement cafés. Just outside the town, there was a three-bedroomed traditional Cretan home on the market for £63,500. It was on two floors, the ground floor being a separate flat, with traditional-sized rooms and splendid views. It would be possible to restore it as one house or to leave the flat separate for visiting friends. 'I thought it was very homely with plenty of possibilites. I loved the tranquillity and the views but it was too modern for me.'

Next she ventured into the foothills of the White Mountains to the village of Fournés, where a 100-year-old Venetian farmhouse was waiting for someone to restore it. It once had five bedrooms, its kitchen and bathroom needed rewiring and replumbing, and the rest needed extensive restoration. It also had plenty of outdoor space plus a few small outbuildings. Priced at £40,500, it would need at least another £14,000 spent on it. Linda could see the potential but felt it would occupy too much

time. 'It's sad because it must have once been such a wonderful place, but it would be too big and expensive a project for me.' A traditional one-bedroomed stone house in Réthymnon almost hit the spot. For £54,000, with an open plan living and dining area, a modern kitchen and bathroom and plenty of outside space, it was tastefully decorated and had the potential for expansion if the garage was converted into a bedroom. 'It was so pretty, especially the courtyard filled with bougainvillea and plant pots. But it only had one bedroom and somehow didn't have the right feel.'

Then Linda saw the house of her dreams. It was in Gavalochóri, a traditional village surrounded by pine and cypress forests and known for its lacemaking, stoneware and bread, which are still made in time-honoured fashion. A modern two-bedroomed house, it had everything Linda wanted for exactly £60,000. It had a spacious living area with high wooden ceilings to ensure it was cool in the summer and warm in the winter, while the main bedroom was a sleeping gallery that extended into the living space. In addition, the current owner's music room could be made into another bedroom. 'I can't keep the smile off my face. You forget it's modern – it's wonderful, so well looked after and the gardens are beautiful.' That week Linda's offer of the asking price was accepted and wheels were put in motion for her move. Twenty-five pounds was enough to enable her to open a bank account and she gave power of attorney to her estate agent so all the transactions could be done without her travelling back and forth.

On returning home, she put her house on the market. It was sold in two weeks, giving her enough to pay for her new home and to have a nest egg in case of emergencies. 'I've begun learning Greek, but they say the best way is to be among the people. I need to research aspects of running a B&B but I've already been asked if I would do some baking for a local bar.' Linda realises just how lucky she is that everything has gone so smoothly. 'I wanted to do this before retiring age so that I could get established and enjoy as many years as possible there. If I had to come back to the UK, I would, but my plan is to spend the rest of my time there.'

'I've begun learning Greek, but they say the best way is to be among the people.'

House-hunters

Chris and Michelle Rhodes

With two older daughters off their hands, sales engineer Chris Rhodes and his wife, Michelle, decided they wanted to start a new life in Greece for themselves and their two-and-a-half-year-old son, Harry. They decided to investigate what the northern part of the Peloponnese peninsula had to offer. 'We want to get out of the rat race and give Harry a better start in life where he can grow up in the sun and have a second language. Our daughters will appreciate the holidays, too.' They didn't have any clear idea of the kind of property they were looking for but knew that they wanted somewhere off the tourist beat where they could lead a quiet life but have access to a town nearby. They had a budget of £90,000, which would derive from the equity raised through the sale of their home plus a local mortgage on the new property.

Their first port of call was near Plátanos where they saw a two-bedroomed flat in a traditional stone house that had been advertised for sale on the internet at £72,000. With a sizeable rear garden, which included several citrus trees and vines, the property had an uninterrupted view down to the coast across green-belt land. 'It was so cool and airy and we liked the fact that it had lots of windows. The downstairs tenant wouldn't put us off because the flat is so self-contained, but the village might be too quiet.'

In contrast, they visited cosmopolitan Pátra. Fifteen minutes outside the town stood a four-bedroomed country home on the market at £82,000. Only 20 years old, it seemed to have everything Chris and Michelle were looking for. 'It's absolutely fantastic. We can't believe how much garden and land come with it. We never expected to get as much as this for our budget.'

Below Despite being over their budget, Chris and Michelle thought this luxury villa was exactly what they were looking for.

Above *An internet advertisement led Chris and Michelle to this apartment in Plátanos.*

Next they went into the mountains to look at a property just outside the village of Kalávrita. For £20,000, they could buy a small two-bedroomed house with a bright pine-panelled living room, a basic kitchen and a big attic space. Small maybe, but it was a knockdown price and had plenty of expansion possibilities. 'It's warm and comfortable. We liked the attic room and the original features such as the panelling and the marble tiles, but it's just too remote for us.' They were concerned that there were no title deeds, despite the reassurance that the local town hall would issue the necessary paperwork (at the extra cost of £1,300 to the Rhodes) because the owner had built the house, lived there for 20 consecutive years and had two witnesses to verify it.

Finally they went to the peaceful seaside village of Selianítika, where they could buy a modern two-bedroomed luxury villa for £127,000. They were able to see the building in progress and appreciate its panoramic views. Looking around a similar completed house, they could see the potential of what they were being offered. 'It's unbelievable. We've seen some nice properties but this is spot-on, with its fantastic touches of luxury and large basement which would make a great playroom for Harry.' It was way over their budget but the developers were prepared to take a £5,000 deposit before completing the first two floors for £90,000, leaving the basement area until Chris and Michelle could afford it.

Torn between the second and fourth properties, they went home to think things over. The visit confirmed in their mind that they wanted to move to Greece but that it was madness to rush into something immediately. They have decided to wait until Chris secures a job there before they move. For the time being, they are learning Greek, maintaining the contacts they have made in the area, and are planning another trip in a few months time to work out the best way to make their dream come true.

'We want to get out of the rat race and give Harry a better start in life, where he can grow up in the sun and have a second language.'

Working out your budget

Buying a property abroad is a big financial commitment so it is important to be aware of your limitations. If you do not think things through from the beginning and allow for the extra costs you will incur on top of the cost of the property, your finances may start to spiral dangerously out of control.

In the first instance, there is the cost of the property itself. You do not have to offer the asking price. In fact, in many countries you are positively expected to haggle before settling on a sum. If you have done your research thoroughly, you will be aware of what similar properties in the area have been sold for and know whether or not you are being asked to pay over the going rate. A good estate agent should be able to advise you whether the owner will entertain a lower offer. If you have had the property looked over by a surveyor or architect, their report may help you negotiate the price down depending on the work needed. Remember to cost in their fees. Some properties are sold complete with furniture. Be very clear what is included in the purchase price and what may need to be negotiated separately.

Apart from the price of the property itself, there are a number of hidden costs directly associated with the purchase that you should be aware of before going ahead. These vary from country to country, but you can expect to add anything between 5 and 15 per cent of the purchase price, depending on where you are. You will have to budget for lawyer's fees. Make sure you are clear what is included in the fee, whether you are being quoted an estimate or the full fee, or whether they charge an hourly rate. It is acceptable to shop around and compare charges if you are worried, but remember that a good solicitor is worth his weight in gold. His fee represents a small amount of the entire purchase and his work can prevent you from making an extremely expensive mistake.

You may also be responsible for notary fees, estate agent's fees, Land Registry fees, transfer tax or stamp duty, search fees, land tax and VAT, depending on where you are buying. These are usually fixed percentages of the purchase price or the declared value of the property. Make sure you know what will be due before you buy. Before moving to some islands in the Caribbean you will have to pay for an Alien Landholder's Licence.

Once the property is bought, your financial outlay is not over. You will need to budget for ongoing annual expenses. These will cover utilities and taxes connected with the property and with your rental income. If you are unclear about what these may be, your lawyer should be able to advise

You will have to budget for an entirely different set of costs if you are buying a plot of land or a derelict house for restoration.

Apart from the price of the property itself, there are a number of hidden costs directly associated with the purchase that you should be aware of before going ahead.

you. If you are taking out a mortgage, you will have to pay an arrangement fee plus the monthly repayments. Remember to include any removal costs. Presumably you will want to insure your property and its contents, too.

Think about the costs of renting the property – you may be paying a letting agency or management company a percentage of the rental income. Even if you are not letting it, you may want to pay a gardener, a pool man or a cleaner to make sure everything is running smoothly in your absence.

You will have to budget for an entirely different set of costs if you are buying a plot of land or a derelict house for restoration. Unless you are going to be there to oversee the work, you will probably want to put the job into the hands of an architect or a project manager. Confirm in writing exactly what their fee covers. The costs of building or restoring a house will depend on all sorts of factors. Be very clear what you can afford and go through every last detail with your architect. Keep in touch all the time to check that costs are being kept within budget. Allow for a contingency sum of at least 10 per cent of the estimated cost, just in case things don't go according to plan. You will also have to budget for connection to the mains utilities and possibly for an access road, depending on how remote your retreat is.

When buying off-plan, make sure you are clear about what is included in the price, right down to the splash-backs and floor tiles. If you specify those you saw in the show home, be aware that they may not be included in the quoted price. Having paid a deposit, you will need to budget for paying the purchase price in stages. Make sure you retain a certain percentage for six months after the property is complete in case of faulty workmanship. If you are in sheltered housing or have bought into a resort complex, you will be contributing to the maintenance of the scheme. Maintenance charges can be extortionate so you must judge whether the facilities provided are worth it. Check exactly what the service charge covers so that you are not hit with unexpected bills over and above it.

If you are moving abroad permanently, you will need to know that your finances will support you long-term. If you are planning to work locally, check that you can get a work permit. Not every country grants them easily. If you are a pensioner moving somewhere other than within the EU or America, you should confirm with the DSS whether you will continue to receive an annual index-linked pension.

Budgeting your purchase is vital. There are all sorts of costs that will be associated with it that you may not have expected. If you take professional advice from the beginning, you should avoid any nasty surprises.

Turkey

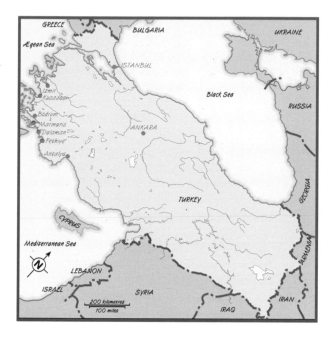

U nsure of whether it belongs to East or West, Turkey is a country unique in its particular blend of cultures. There are thousands of ancient historical sites to explore, including the great classical ruins of the ancient cities of Ephesus and Troy; natural marvels such as the gleaming white, calcium-rich pools of Pammukkale; the architectural marvels of Istanbul, especially the mosques of the architect Sinan; and the Byzantine splendours of Edirne.

The whole place is infused with the spirit of Greek mythology and legend – indeed, many classical Greek archaeological sites are to be found in Turkey. You will experience a fascinating mix of the old and new in a climate that promises seven months of coastal sunshine and the romance of living in a country that in some places seems hardly to have been affected by the passing of time. As you wake in the morning to clear summer skies and the sound of the *muezzin* calling the faithful to prayer, you will know that you have entered a different culture. The Aegean and Mediterranean coasts offer great beaches and famously turquoise seas. Inland, you will find vast oak and pine forests, shimmering lakes and wide, green plains. Over recent years, the coastline has been greatly developed for tourism and there is a growing interest in buying holiday homes here.

Turkey is a huge nation bordered on three sides by the Black Sea, the Aegean Sea and the Mediterranean. In the east, it has frontiers with Armenia, Georgia, Iran, Iraq and Syria. Known in ancient times as Asia Minor, the region has been a 'cradle of civilisations' but its history has been volatile – the scene of countless invasions and migrations. Ethnic conflicts still exist and some parts of the country are quite lawless, particularly in the eastern hinterland where the Kurds have been fighting for their independence. The Turkish government's ambition to join the European Union may one day be realised. Before that happens, Turkey will have to improve its human rights record. The infrastructure of the country as a whole is still far from matching western European standards. This is less noticeable in the coastal areas, where the tourist developments are booming, and in the principal cities, although the cost of living remains about a third of that in the UK.

With airports at Istanbul, Izmir, Bodrum, Antalya and Dalaman, the coastal regions are just four hours from the UK. If you want to travel within the country, the long-distance coach has become part of modern Turkish culture. In the towns, *dolmus*, shared taxis plying a fixed route, operate.

Turkey is known for its bazaars. These are large market places, usually warrens of narrow streets where traders of different merchandise (rugsellers, goldsmiths, spice merchants) noisily tout for business. The best-known is Istanbul's Karpali Çarsi, which has miles of streets each named after the trade to be found there. But even the smallest town has its market place where you will inevitably be invited to bargain but are unlikely ever to best the seller.

Turkish cuisine relies on fresh ingredients in imaginative combinations and includes many grains and pulses. Dishes are rich, spicy and varied because of the cultural mix. A meal might begin with *mezze* – a huge variety of hors d'oevres, including *dolmades* (stuffed vine leaves), *patlican salatsi* (aubergne purée), *cacik* (yoghurt and cucumber), *imam bayeldi* (aubergine, onion, tomato and garlic) and *pilaki* (white beans and onions). There is plenty of freshly caught fish available. Some favourites are red mullet, swordfish, bluefish and bass, which are often served simply grilled. Lamb is used in most meat dishes such as döner or shish kebabs, meatballs or more substantial stews. The Turks have a sweet tooth – their best known dessert is *baklava*, layers of sticky filo pastry soaked in honey. For those who prefer something less sickly, there's always *krem karamel* or lashings of fresh fruit.

Istanbul is the old imperial capital of Turkey. Despite Ankara taking over as its modern counterpart, Istanbul still retains its position as the commercial and cultural centre of Turkey, and remains the focus for many tourists who come to savour its undisputable charms. With its distinct skyline of minarets and domes, some of its legacies from its diverse history as capital to both Christian and Islamic Empires are immediately evident. Since 1984, the city has been undergoing a renaissance. Schemes to restore Istanbul have been put in place, with the development of new parks and museums alongside renovations of the older quarters.

The city is divided into north and south by the Golden Horn. This separates the Byzantine and Ottoman walled city from the old Genoese quarter of Beyoglu, from which spreads Istanbul's commercial centre. The Straits of Bosphorus connects the Black Sea with the Sea of Marmara – East with West. Smart suburbs line the Bosphorus where western Europeans tend to set up home. This is an incredibly fast-growing city. Extensive shanty towns occupy the outskirts thanks to a law which gave immediate squatters' rights to those putting up shelter on public ground under cover of night – a strategy not recommended for expatriates, however low the budget.

The most popular destinations for British homebuyers lie along the Aegean and Mediterranean coasts where they can be assured of clear seas, a warm climate and a relaxed way of life.

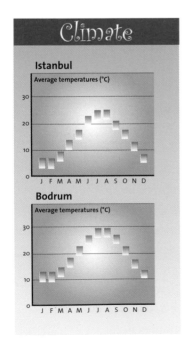

Climate

Istanbul
Average temperatures (°C)

Bodrum
Average temperatures (°C)

86 . . . . *A Place in the Sun*

Left Wooden-fronted houses overlook the Bosphorus in Istanbul's suburb of Ermigan.

Izmir is the third largest town in Turkey after Istanbul and Ankara, and the second largest port after Istanbul. It lacks the historic dimension of other towns because it was devasted by fire and looting after Turkey's victory over the Greeks in 1922 – the Turks set alight the large Greek and Armenian sectors, destroying much of the city and killing thousands of non-Muslims. Now rebuilt, Izmir is dramatically located round a huge bay circled by mountains. It is a modern city with wide palm-lined boulevards, a vibrant atmosphere and plenty of cafés, quayside restaurants and museums; it also has a lively, but typically labyrinthine, bazaar. The hill behind the town is topped by Kadifekale, the Velvet Castle, which dominates the town. Legend has it that Nemesis appeared to Alexander the Great here and told him to build a town on this spot. Whatever its true origins, Izmir is certainly a great stepping off point for exploring the region.

Beyond the rich agricultural land to the west of the city lies the Çesme peninsula, which, despite its barren landscape, is a rapidly growing resort area. Tourism has transformed Çesme from a small fishing village into an enchanting seaside town, attracting visitors to its talcum beaches and annual Sea Festival. Behind the harbour, old Greek houses gather beneath the Genoese fortress in narrow streets where old craftsmen still ply their trades. Apart from the region's attractions of white beaches and azure waters, most particularly at Altınkum, it also boasts unspoilt fishing villages such as Dalyan and Sığacık; the marina town of Ilıca, which is famed for its thermal baths; and the ancient ruins of Teos, Erytherai and, most famously, Ephesus – the largest, best-preserved ancient city in the Mediterranean. Kusadası is also a well-established popular resort. Inland, there are plenty of towns and villages where life goes on much as it has for many years. The pace is slow – women can be seen sewing rugs while men herd the flocks or tend the olive groves, tobacco, grain and cotton fields, or simply sit in the shade of a village square.

Further south, another magnet for potential British homebuyers is the area around Bodrum. The town's origins date back thousands of years to when it was known as Halikarnassos, the capital of the Carian empire, and later the birthplace of Herodotus. It was the first resort to be developed in Turkey and is now one of most popular. Its square white houses gleam under the sun as they retreat from the busy port and marina. The town is dominated by the imposing 15th-century castle of St Peter, which sits on a promontory dividing the two bays around which Bodrum is built. The relaxed

atmosphere is cosmopolitan in flavour with plenty of restaurants, bars and clubs.

If you want somewhere quieter, with more traditional Turkish character, then it is worth exploring the rest of the Bodrum peninsula, greener in the north than the rugged south. Before the end of the Turkish War of Independence, the population here was mostly Greek and they have left an indelible impression with windmills, churches (now dilapidated) and typical stone houses. There are still unspoilt and tranquil villages to be found such as Akyarlar, Bitez, Gölköy, Güvercinlik and Gümüslük, each with their own appeal. Out to sea, there are numerous tiny islands: Karaada, famous for its mud baths; Kargacık Bükü, a popular holiday resort; and Cedreae, which is is believed to be the trysting place of Anthony and Cleopatra. All watersports fanatics and sun-lovers will find themselves quite at home around here.

Marmaris, another popular town, is known for its splendidly dramatic setting by a deep gorge that is flanked with pine-clad hills. It has good amenities and facilities, a lively buzz in the air and is home to Turkey's largest marina. The old town is built on different levels that twist around a 16th-century citadel. In the summer, when the place is crowded and noisy, you can escape into the mountainous interior of the Hisarönü peninsula towards the quieter towns of Selimiye, Bozburun or Bayır. Here you can sip tea in the main square beneath an ancient pine tree. The road from Marmaris twists down the Datça peninsula – with sea views glimpsed through the pine woods – until it reaches the boat-building centre of Datça itself, a quiet town with one main street and a fine harbour with teahouses, restaurants and bars. As the peninsula widens, almond and olive groves crowd sleepy villages sheltering at the foot of the mountains. At the tip, the remains of the ancient city of Knidos look out to sea, recalling better days when it was a prosperous port known throughout the region.

Millions of British holidaymakers visit the south-west coast of Turkey every year, so it's surprising that there are not more people buying holiday homes there. It's a beautiful, very friendly part of the world where you can get excellent value for your money. Recently, the devaluation of the Turkish lira has meant that real property bargains can be found. This is where the snow-capped Toros mountains drop to the sea, giving a heroic backdrop to the coastline. Here the rock colour is so pale and the water so clear that it looks a perfect blue, hence the name, Turquoise Coast. Until the

Above *Despite its popularity as a
tourist resort, Fethiye has managed
to retain its identity as a lively
market town.*

1970s, many of the glorious beaches were only accessible by sea so it became a popular
destination for the yachting community. But with the construction of a new main road
from Marmaris to Antalya, the way has been opened for development. However,
planning regulations are strict, limiting the height of buildings and protecting areas
of archaeological interest.

Fethiye is the main resort town of the Turquoise Coast. Everything centres on the
harbour, where a pleasant evening can be enjoyed in one of the many restaurants. The
pedestrianised old town is a maze of little streets with shops selling rugs, jewellery and
spices. The Gulf of Fethiye is dotted with 12 small islands that protect the town from
storms but whose many coves also provide secret hideaways from the summer crowds.
Other good beaches nearby are at Çalış, Gemiler, Kidrak and Ölüdeniz. Almost 5,000
years ago this was the mountainous terrain of the Lycians, a race who left, among other
legacies, the extraordinary rock tombs that can still be seen throughout the region.

Ölüdeniz, famous for its lagoon and spectacular setting of pine forests tumbling
down to the waters, is just a stone's throw along the coast. Extremely popular in the
summer, it has a crowded party atmosphere. However, retreat into the green belt
area of the plateau behind and you will find peace and quiet, and a welcome cool breeze
taking the edge off the summer heat. If the beach and lagoon are too crowded, then
there are always the neighbouring beaches of Belcegiz or Kidrak.

Not far inland from Fethiye is the abandoned ghost town of Kaya Köyü. It was left
deserted when its Orthodox Greek inhabitants were deported after a population
exchange between Greece and Turkey in a deal overseen by the League of Nations
following the Turkish War of Independence in 1923. Many Turks sent to live here did
not stay because they believed a curse had been put on the place. For years, the once
prosperous town stood almost empty and crumbling to the ground until an
enterprising developer, realising there were no title deeds to the buildings, saw an
opportunity and planned to bring it back to life. In response, the Ministry of Culture
swiftly declared the town a protected zone where only approved restoration is allowed.

Kaya Köyü has recently been declared a 'Peace Village' and is a symbol of the improving relationship between Greece and Turkey. The EU and Greece have donated large sums of money so that the two churches in the village can be restored, and, in time, a school and a few cottages will also be renovated.

All along the coast there are many ancient city sites to be explored – at Tlos, Pinara, Sidyma, Letöon, Xanthos and Patara to name but a few. Patara also has the benefit of a spectacular, long sandy beach that is closed in the evening so that the rare loggerhead turtles can come uninterrupted to lay their eggs. Pine-clad mountains are the backdrop to a dramatic coastline punctured by steep gorges and fertile plains. It is believed that St Nicholas (Father Christmas) was born at Patara; he subsequently lived in Demre where he became the patron saint of sailors.

Above Kalkan boasts good shopping, top-class restaurants and first-rate spearfishing opportunities out to sea.

Today a tiny church is dedicated to his memory, with a shrine and museum.

Kalkan is a charming old fishing village built on a hill overlooking the harbour. The old stone houses hang precariously on to the steep slope, their wooden balconies jutting above the narrow windy streets. Its companion town, Kas, just along the coast, has been transformed into an upmarket resort where luxury yachts replace the old fishing boats in the harbours and smart boutiques line the cobbled streets. Like so many towns it has a large bazaar with shops selling carpets, leather goods, jewellery and all kinds of local crafts and produce. Both towns are blessed with a selection of bars and restaurants that provide a lively night life.

Another extremely popular town with British homeowners is Antalya, the principal city on the Mediterranean coast and the fastest growing city in Turkey. Set high on a fertile plateau, it is surrounded on three sides by mountains and on the fourth by a clean coastline that is punctured by streams and waterfalls that rush towards the sea. The town is surrounded by agricultural land where everything is grown, from watermelons and flowers to vegetables, citrus fruits and cotton. Every watersport is on offer but inland there are also opportunities for caving, climbing, trekking and even skiing. The city itself has a history stretching back to the second century BC, when it was founded by Attalus II, King of Pergamum. It has since become a thriving modern centre separated from the old quarter, Kaleiçi, by Roman walls. Declared a conservation area, many of the traditional wooden houses of Kaleiçi that crowd the winding streets leading down to the busy Roman harbour have been restored. The main point of reference is the Yivli Minare, a handsome fluted minaret, just down the hill from the clock tower and close to the Fortress Gate. Outside the town there are numerous archaeological remains, including Termessus, Olimpos, Perge and Aspendos.

It's only possible to give a taste of the many delights to be found in modern Turkey. It is a country moving forward thanks to its new popularity as a tourist destination and the government's desire to become a member of the EU. Buying property here is relatively inexpensive and, if chosen carefully, may be regarded as a good investment for the future.

How to get there

Air
Turkish Airlines and British Airways fly directly from Heathrow to Istanbul, Antalya, Ankara, Dalaman and Izmir. Charter flights are also available.
Flight time: 4–7 hours

A Place in the Sun

How to buy property in... Turkey

There are strict rules for foreigners buying property in Turkey, so it essential you consult a bilingual lawyer who will handle the details of your purchase for you since it is only possible to give general information here. Your lawyer is necessary at every stage because any infringement of the law could have serious consequences. He will know the various restrictions that must be observed depending on the property. Zoning restrictions mean foreigners cannot buy land in a military or security zone, in certain villages, or outside the boundaries of a municipality, though it may be possible to get round this by establishing a company.

Having negotiated hard over the price for your property (there tend to be no market values) you can proceed to an initial contract which must contain all the relevant details of the buyer and seller and all conditional clauses which will cover you in the event of such things as there not being clear title, there being debts on the property, or your inability to secure a loan on it. A deposit of 10–25 per cent is paid at this stage and is forfeited if you do not complete the purchase. It is vital your lawyer conducts extensive searches since, for example, it possible to buy a property with a debt, for which you will become responsible.

Generally, one notary acts for both buyer and seller and is obliged to act with impartiality. However, the notary is not reponsible for registering the transfer of property. This must be done by an official of the Property Registry department in the presence of both buyer and seller. The original deeds are sent to Ankara and you should receive copies the same day. At this point the balance of the purchase price plus all taxes, duties and registration fees are due to be paid. Find out exactly what these are likely to be before you buy. Expect them to be higher than in the UK and budget for anything between 12 and 15 per cent of the purchase price. The main taxes are a buyer's and seller's tax of around 4.5 per cent each. Who pays them is negotiable. Subsequently there is a 0.4 per cent annual property tax to be paid which is reassesed every four years.

Because the purchase and rental of property by foreigners is a relatively recent phenomenon, it is recommended that you seek advice from the local British Consulate as to how to proceed without mishap. Ask your lawyer to explain Turkish inheritance laws. They are very different from British laws and may have significant repercussions if you do not take them into account before signing any contract.

Useful Addresses

Turkish Consulate General
Rutland Lodge,
Rutland Gardens
London SW7 1BW
Tel: 020 7589 0949

Turkish Embassy
43 Belgrave Square
London
SW1X 8PA
Tel: 020 7393 0202

Turkish Tourist Office
170–173 Piccadilly
London W1V 9DD
Tel: 020 7355 4207

24-hour visa information
service 0906 834 7348

House-hunters

> ‘We came over the mountain and saw this beautiful vista spread in front of us and immediately thought, “Yes!”’

Tim Levingston and Bridget Ives

As his 50th birthday loomed, sales director Tim Levingston and his partner, marketing consultant Bridget Ives, decided it was time to do something different with their lives. ‘I’d been in the IT industry for 31 years and we had a generally pleasant lifestyle in Tring, but for some years I’d been too aware that life isn’t a rehearsal and we wanted a change.’ The impetus was provided unexpectedly by a call from his daughter on holiday in Turkey, announcing her intended marriage to a local man. Tim and Bridget decided to fly out to meet him. Staying in Fethiye’s Hotel Letoonia, overlooking the bay, they recognised the potential of this stunning, but under-developed, area and within a week of returning home, their house was on the market.

Having already explored the possibilities of earning a living by renting holiday accommodation, they returned four months later to research more thoroughly and to explore the coast one hour’s drive either side of Dalaman airport.

‘We eventually came back to the Fethiye area because it was, strangely, the most beautiful and yet the least developed. Originally, we had imagined buying three Provençal-type farmhouses to renovate but there seemed to be nothing but expensive, newly built villas or concrete blocks with reinforcing rods sticking out. Eventually someone suggested we went to the Kaya Köyü valley. We came over the mountain and saw this beautiful vista spread in front of us and immediately thought, “Yes!” We put the word around and found a plot of land which was exactly the right size for four villas and in a spectacular position.’

The English couple who owned the land had bought it in the name of their lawyer because of the zoning restrictions that preclude foreigners from purchasing property outside the municipalities. Nonetheless, this is something to be wary of doing because legally speaking it did not actually belong to the owners. To get around this restriction, Tim and Bridget brought in a top consultant from Ankara who advised them to set up a foreign capital company. This requires two partners (Tim and Bridget) and an initial investment of $US50,000 each (less than they were proposing to spend on the property).

‘We started the process from the UK but singularly failed to get the written details of the planning regulations from the local authorities. In the end, my daughter got married in Ankara in April 1998, so we put our remaining furniture in storage and left the UK for good. After the wedding we stayed in a small apartment for a few weeks and, with the help of our consultant, sorted out the building regs, bought a house in Fethiye, the land and a car, and suddenly everything fell into place.’

Below Tim and Bridget on the terrace of the Villa Camellia, one of the villas they rent out.

Tim and Bridget then had to embark on building their villas. They had been fortunate in finding a bilingual architect – 'a must' – and took a month to write a fixed-price, staged-payments contract with a firm of local builders. The contract was to build four villas and a swimming pool, and was written to ensure the builders were motivated to progress the work as quickly as possible. Eight months later, in January 1999, Tim and Bridget moved into their very own house on a building site. 'We wanted to do the gardens ourselves but it rained till March. We designed them, then landscape gardeners responsible for the Letoonia's gardens put down the top soil, sowed the grass seed and planted 60 trees and 2,000 plants and shrubs. Our first guests arrived in July and we've never looked back.' Tim and Bridget are now successfully renting out their villas to holidaymakers via their website, www.turkeyvillas.com.

When pressed, Tim admits that he does miss his golf and English beer, but the pros far outweigh the cons. 'We've had a tough two years but we'd never go back now. The climate and the scenery are huge factors in our being here. And, let's face it, working for seven months out of 12 isn't bad, especially when part of that work involves chatting to people round the pool and taking them out to supper.'

Above and below Nearby Fethiye provided an ideal base for Tim and Bridget while their new home (below) and the other three villas were built.

Getting a mortgage

If you are moving abroad permanently, the sale of your house in the UK may release sufficient capital to pay for your new home. If you are paying in cash, investigate the best way to transfer the money to the country in question, taking into account the exchange rate and the optimum time and place to exchange it. You will need to open a bank account in the country to which you are moving and obtain a certificate of importation for the money you bring in with you. This will make it easier to repatriate your money if you decide to move to another country later. Seek advice from your bank manager or an independent financial advisor. If you are less fortunate and need to borrow money for your property, it is essential to take professional advice.

There are several routes you can take if you need to borrow money to complete your purchase. To help you choose the right one, it is important to talk to an impartial financial advisor and your lawyer. Make absolutely certain that any purchase contract you sign includes a conditional clause making clear your offer is subject to your obtaining a mortgage.

In many countries you will be able to take out a mortgage with a local bank or with a local branch of a British bank or building society. Many people prefer this type of arrangement because it keeps their affairs in a different country quite separate. When arranging a mortgage abroad, shop around to see who is offering the best terms, taking into

consideration the set-up fees, the percentage they will lend on the property (usually between 60 and 80 per cent) and the interest rate they will charge on the loan. The term of a European or Caribbean loan is usually 15 years, whereas in America it can be up to 30 years. You should be prepared to provide proof of income and supply copies of three months' payslips, your P60 and six months' worth of bank statements. If you are self-employed, be prepared to produce your last three years of audited accounts and six months' worth of bank statements. The potential lender is also likely to take into account your existing liabilities such as current mortgage arrangements, outstanding credit card debts and standing orders, and will expect these plus the new mortgage payments to represent a fixed percentage of your regular income.

If you are depending on rental income to pay off your mortgage, you should check that lenders in the country of your choice will take that into account. In countries that do not (for example, France, Portugal and Italy) you will be limited in the amount of money you can raise. Not all lenders will insist on a survey, as they do in the UK, although it would be sensible to have one carried out independently for your own peace of mind. Some countries (such as France, Portugal and some Caribbean islands) insist that a suitable life assurance is assigned to the lender and home insurance is taken out.

You will need to find out the date the

There are several routes you can take if you need to borrow money to complete your purchase. To help you choose the right one, it is important to talk to an impartial financial advisor and your lawyer.

property will be registered in your name because the lender will not usually lend against the security of the property until that time. In Spain, for example, you will have to acquire a *nota simple* to verify you will have full title to the property before a lender will consider an evaluation of the property. If you take out a mortgage in another currency, you must take into account possible fluctuations in that currency which may affect your repayments. You should also take professional advice regarding the tax and inheritance implications inherent in taking out a mortgage in another country.

Mortgages in America can also be secured from a number of different sources, all of which will scrutinise your financial status. It may be worth comparing advantages of both a UK and US mortgage as there could be tax advantages. Most foreigners can obtain US loans of up to 80 per cent of the purchase price and these are normally repaid over a 30-year term regardless of age, although be prepared to pay 1 per cent more interest than a US citizen, as you will be treated as an investor.

It is important to understand that every country has different requirements when it comes to securing a mortgage. It is essential you take the appropriate professional advice and know exactly what will be expected of you and the implications of the decision you make.

Rather than taking out a separate mortgage on the new property, you may feel it is simpler to take out a home equity loan from your current mortgage lender in the UK. This will be secured against the equity you have in your existing property. Such an arrangement will enable you, as a cash buyer, to purchase your new home abroad outright.

Offshore companies operate from various tax havens around the world. Using one can be a tax efficient way of buying a property. Opening an account may require a sizeable minimum deposit and balance, and it may operate restrictive and punitive terms and conditions. It is important to check the credit rating of the financial institution you choose in the interest of protecting your money. This can be a costly process, but in Portugal, for example, some lenders will only deal through the medium of an offshore company. The advantages of such an arrangement are that you will be exempt from local taxes and inheritance laws. In France, it is possible to buy property through the SCI (Société Civile Immobilière), another tax-efficient means. If you are contemplating going down this route, seek expert legal and financial advice to explain the ramifications.

When seeking advice, take the sensible precaution of consulting a company that is a member of FOPDAC (The Federation of Overseas Property Developers, Agents and Consultants). FOPDAC was established in 1973 to protect the interests of people buying or selling a property overseas and its member companies must conform with the Federation's strict code of ethics.

Cyprus

Cyprus is a captivating island of spectacular contrasts. A popular destination for British homebuyers, it offers sun-drenched beaches, clear azure waters, traditional mountain villages, modern resorts, Byzantine churches and extraordinary sites of antiquity. It has a rich history with a wide diversity of cultures that have influenced its development over the centuries.

In 1960, Britain relinquished sovereignty and the republic of Cyprus was born. But relations between the Turks and Greeks were uneasy and in 1974, Turkey invaded the northern part of the island. The subsequent division between the Greek Republic of Cyprus in the south and the Turkish Republic of Northern Cyprus was established. Tourist facilities on the Turkish side of the island have been less developed than those in Greek Cyprus, which has been a magnet for tourists ever since. The most popular resort areas are centred on Larnaka, Lemesos and Páfos on the south coast. Inland, the mountains of the Troödos Massif, cloaked in pine, cedar and juniper forests, are cool and inviting. They offer great opportunities for walkers and cyclists, and Mount Olympus has the island's only ski resort. A country steeped in mythology, with hospitable people, a reliable climate and the gentle sound of the bouzouki in the air – who could want for more?

Capital Lefkosia (Nicosia)
Population 758,000
Land area 9,250 sq km (of which 3,355 sq km are in the Turkish Cypriot area)
Currency Greek Cypriot area: 1 Cypriot pound = 100 cents; Turkish Cypriot area: 1 Turkish lira (TL) = 100 kurus
Electricity 240v
Time zone GMT + 2 hours
Religion Predominantly Greek Orthodox
Language Greek, Turkish, English
Government Republic

Many British people are drawn by the promise of the sunniest island in the Mediterranean and opt to have second homes in the Greek Republic of Cyprus. Communications are generally good, with two international airports at Larnaka and Páfos. The routes between the coastal resorts are well-maintained, but further inland they can be much more basic and you will need a car to get around. The cost of living is not too high, the people are generous and welcoming and the crime rate is low. The climate is agreeable and air pollution is almost non-existent. Cyprus has proved an ideal place for retirement. It is not just the relaxed and comfortable lifestyle that beckons. Foreign residents are also attracted by the duty-free facilities, low taxation on any income they may have from abroad, and the benefits to be had from the double tax treaty. Medical services on Cyprus are first-rate and there are a wide range of schools, some of which follow English or American curricula.

Living in Cyprus has plenty to offer – and not least the food. Situated at the crossroads of the Levant, the cuisine of the island has been subjected to Mediterranean and Middle Eastern influences. There is fresh fruit and vegetables in abundance, delicious local bread and pastries, and much local wine to sample. The favourite meal comes *mezze*-style: a series of small dishes which are served until you are full. They may include local cheese such as halloumi or feta, *houmous* (chick pea dip), octopus, shrimps, stuffed vine leaves, local sausage, olives and smoked ham. Other local specialities include *fasolada*, the national dish of beans, *afélia* (pork with wine and coriander), *avgolemoni patcha* (lamb stew with lemon) and game dishes. The Cypriots also love sweets so be on the lookout for delicious treats such as glacéed fruit, varieties of honey cakes and little pancake wraps.

The wine of Cyprus is mentioned in the Bible and the wine-making traditions have been continued ever since. A sweet red dessert wine, Commandaria, was drunk by the Crusaders and purports to be the oldest wine in the world. A considerable range of labels are to be found for red, white and rosé wines, but the island also produces its own sherry, vermouth and port. Zivánia is the local hooch; it may be flavoured with spices but it still has the kick of a mule. Brandy is also produced, and has become the national tipple, particularly when knocked back as a brandy sour – mixed with lemon or lime and bitters.

The capital of the Greek Republic of Cyprus is Lefkosia, formerly Nicosia, the only city in the world that is strictly divided – in this case between the Republican south and the Turkish north. The division is marked by the 'Green Line', so-called because the British military recorded the division with green ink on a map, which is physically characterised by bunkers.

Southern Lefkosia is a vibrant city with plenty of good restaurants, shopping and historical sites. The old city is surrounded by imposing Venetian ramparts that were built in the 16th century. They are punctuated by the famous Páfos and Famagusta gates, which invite visitors in from the modern city outside. The walls themselves are used variously as car parks, outdoor concert spaces and pleasant promenades. Inside the walls lies Laïki Geitonia, a carefully restored area of narrow stone streets with small museums and churches, craft shops, tavernas, the smell of cooking, and brilliant flowers tumbling from pots everywhere. In the summer, the city can be extremely hot, which is one of the reasons why most homebuyers head for the coast.

The international airport is on the south coast, conveniently close to Larnaka. Larnaka is the second port of the island and provides anchorage for yachts and motor boats from all over the Mediterranean. Thanks to a recent facelift, the long, palm-lined promenade that skirts the harbour is lined with stylish cafés and bars. The city itself was built on the site of Kition, a flourishing port from Phoenician times onwards. The only section of the old town that is visible now is to the north of the city, where the archaeological site is known as Area 2. Supposedly, Christianity came early to Kition in the shape of Lazarus, newly resurrected by Jesus, who arrived here to become the first Bishop of Cyprus and, eventually, its patron saint. His tomb is believed to be in the church of Áyios Lázaros although his remains were removed in the ninth century. The town has seen many changes since his day and is now a pleasant, relatively restful place to spend time. The beaches close to the town are mediocre but further east there are plenty of excellent stretches of sand. However, the resorts are very busy, especially Ayía Nápa.

Inland from Ayía Nápa are the red villages, or Kokkinohoriá, so-called because of the colour of the bricks made from the local earth. It is also a region famed for its potato production. To the west of Larnaka are the glistening salt lake and the Hala Sultan Tekke, a seventh-century mosque that attracts many Muslim pilgrims. Other sights in the area include the Chapelle Royale, a small church dedicated to St Catherine, and the Stavrovoúni Monastery, which is perched high on an overhanging crag. It is the oldest monastery in Cyprus and was founded by St Helena, the mother of the Roman Emperor Constantine. It is said that she brought a piece of the true cross here.

The highlight of the region must be the village of Lefkara. For hundreds of years it has been an important centre for exquisite lacemaking and silver-smithing – even Leonardo da Vinci is supposed to have once bought an altar cloth before returning home to Italy. Many of the old houses have been restored and give far better value for money than properties found by the coast. Stone houses, with their distinctive orange-tiled roofs and balconies hung with lacework, and the narrow streets, make Lefkara an obvious attraction.

Richard the Lionheart first brought Cyprus to the attention of the English in the 12th century. He was on his way to the Crusades when his sister and his bride-to-be,

Below Sheltered by the foothills of the Troödos mountains, Lefkara is an idyllic mountain hamlet but only 20 minutes by car to Lemesos or Larnaka.

Above The centre of Páfos still has the charm of an old fishing village with a quayside lined with fish restaurants and cafés.

Berengaria of Navarre, were threatened by the Byzantine governor of Cyprus. Richard immediately detoured to the island to capture it and eventually sell it to Guy de Lusignan, but not before he had married Berengaria in Lemesos (Limassol). Now, it is the largest port in the Greek Republic of Cyprus and attracts a huge number of tourists and expatriate homebuyers.

When Famagusta and Kyrenia were occupied by Turkish troops in 1974, Lemesos fast expanded into the commercial centre of the south, with restaurants, luxury hotels and resort complexes springing up. There is a tradition of hospitality in the town, which is extended during the riotous carnival week in February and the wine festival in September. The old part of the town is crowded with Levantine stone buildings lining narrow lanes that circle the restored medieval castle and museum. Elsewhere in the town there are plenty of cafés, bars and restaurants to while away the hours. The miles of beautiful beaches around Lemesos are known as the 'Cypriot Riviera', which stretches from Governor Beach to Avdimou Beach and Pissouri Bay.

The district of Lemesos is hilly and fertile with all sorts of fruit trees (citrus, cherry, pear, peach, plum, avocado, fig, pomegranate) growing beside vineyards, olive groves and vegetable patches. For those escaping the cities or looking for an idyllic home abroad, small villages offer splendid opportunities for the restoration of houses. The main attractions of the region are: Amathous, one of the ancient city-kingdoms of Cyprus where, allegedly, Ariadne fled from the Cretan labyrinth; Kolossi Castle; the Sanctuary of Apollon Ylatis; and, most spectacular of all, Kourion, the cliff-top site of an ancient city that is dominated by an amphitheatre.

For those wanting a quieter, more traditional Cypriot experience, Páfos and the western end of the island are an ideal place. This region has the best climate on the island, with short-lived mild winters and day after day of sunshine the rest of the year.

100 . . . . *A Place in the Sun*

The delightful western coastal town of Páfos is built around an attractive harbour filled with brightly coloured fishing and pleasure boats. The vibrant, atmospheric part of lower Páfos contrasts with the elegance of upper Pafos, where boulevards are flanked by palm trees and classical-style buildings.

St Paul allegedly converted the first ruler of Cyprus to Christianity in Páfos, but the town has a much steamier reputation as the centre of the love cult of Aphrodite. Aphrodite was the Greek goddess of sexual love and legend has it that she rose from the sea covered in foam on the spot where Aphrodite's Rock rears up from the sea outside Páfos. It is said that anyone swimming around the rock will be granted the gift of eternal youth. The Baths of Aphrodite are out of town in a secluded spot where the goddess supposedly came to bathe after entertaining her lovers. The remains of her earliest sanctuary are at Kouklia.

Páfos has a rich history and so many treasures have been unearthed there that it has been added to UNESCO's World Heritage list. There are the stunning collection of mosaics in the houses of Dionysus, Theseus and Aion which have been unearthed after 16 centuries; the sprawling tombs and chambers of the Tombs of the Kings; the pillar to which St Paul was allegedly tied and whipped; and the ancient Odeon theatre. Still other treasures are displayed in the Archaeological and Byzantine museums.

Outside the town, the countryside is cultivated with banana plantations, with the foothills of the Troödos mountains as a backdrop. Many of the old houses have been restored in Peyía, an attractive village overlooking the sea and another popular choice for homebuyers. This is just the first in a series of pretty inland villages – Kathikas, Pano Akourdalia, Kato Akourdalia, Inia or Goudi – all of which have wonderful views, peace, quiet and cooler temperatures. Local vineyards supply good wine to accompany your *mezze*.

To the north west, the Akamas Peninsula has been recently established as a national park. It is cut with spectacular gorges and offers excellent walking trails, a huge variety of flora and fauna and some of the best beaches on the island. The peaceful resort of Polis on the north coast overlooks the stunning Chrysochou Bay and the unspoilt

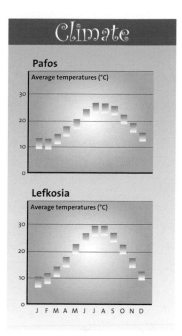

Climate

Pafos
Average temperatures (°C)

Lefkosia
Average temperatures (°C)

J F M A M J J A S O N D

Left *To the north of Páfos there are plenty of opportunities to find a dream home in one of the developed villages along the coast, such as Coral Bay.*

Above *Wine lovers will feel at home among the villages of the Troödos foothills where Omodhos is renowned as Cyprus's wine capital.*

How to get there

Air
British Airways flies from Heathrow to Larnaka. Cyprus Airways flies from Gatwick Heathrow and Stansted to Larnaka and Páfos. Air 2000 flies from Gatwick and Stansted to Páfos, from Gatwick to Larnaka. Charter flights are available but often difficult to obtain because they tend to be tied up with the package companies.
Flight time: 4–4½ hours

fishing village of Latsi. The foothills of the Troödos mountains offer majestic scenery, particularly in Cedar Valley, which is home to the island's very own horned sheep, the moufflon. The Páfos region is one that yields plenty of rewards, whether it's history, nature, beaches, watersports, hiking or just a quiet, relaxed way of life.

Cyprus has much more to offer than beach life. The Troödos mountain range, which stretches across the centre of Cyprus, provides a completely different experience. Not only are fantastic views and pine-scented breezes to be found in abundance, its highest point, Mount Olympus, is also home to the island's only ski resort. For the more energetic, it is possible to ski in the morning and be on the beach in the afternoon in time for a dip. Hidden in the pine forests are many Byzantine churches. There are monasteries there, too, most notably the Maheras Monastery in the southern foothills, and Kykkos Monastery on the edge of the Marathasa Valley.

However, the mountains have not only provided a safe haven for religious communities; in days gone by, they have also offered a cool alternative to the heat of the coast for wealthy Cypriots and Turks. There are delightful villages to be found. One of the best known is Platres, which has long been a popular getaway. It was modelled on the colonial Indian hill stations and its original villas echo the Raj style. Rustic life is unhurried and the people are hospitable and courteous. Many villages are known for a particular craft or product: Pródromos is famous for its apples; Omodhos for its wine; Fini for its pottery and *loukoumi* (little shortbreads); Redoulas for its cherries; and Mouroullas for its carved wooden bowls. There's no shortage of things to do up here – hikers and mountain bikers are presented with first-rate challenges, horse riders can take to the saddle, wine lovers can visit the wineries in the Pitsylia region, local history buffs can visit the pretty preserved villages of Fikardou and Lazania, and botanists and bird watchers will be in seventh heaven. The more sedate can relax by one of Platres' three swimming pools or sit in the shade of a taverna and watch the world go by.

How to buy property in...
Cyprus

The procedure for buying property in Cyprus is very similar to the British purchase process. However, there are differences so make sure you take professional advice to avoid any pitfalls. These are the basic steps you will need to take.

First, you must engage a lawye, either in Cyprus or the UK, who will draw up the contract and see to the conveyancing. It is important to discuss with your lawyer which conditional clauses should be included. These cover items such as your ability to obtain the necessary government permits, planning permission, clear title, and due confirmation of the boundaries. They also allow for the discovery of restrictive covenants or negative results of a survey, and the itemising of furniture that the vendor has agreed to sell. When this preliminary contract is signed, it binds the buyer and seller to the terms they have agreed. This is subject to the purchaser obtaining the necessary government permits and clear title to the property.

At this stage a deposit – usually 10 per cent – will be lodged with the lawyer who will carry out the searches at the District Land Registry. Title deeds have provided problems in the past so you are advised not to part with any cash until you are certain they are available. Property in the country may have more than one owner so it's essential that you have the agreement of all parties to the sale.

Foreign nationals have to apply to the Council of Ministers before they can buy a property. Essentially this is just a formality and is due to be banned for EU nationals, but it can take some time – sometimes longer than a year.

The contract is lodged with the Land Registry to prevent the property being sold from under your nose. This is the moment to apply to the Central Bank for a permit to transfer the necessary funds. When the searches have been satisfactorily completed, check that the property is in the condition in which you last saw it and that you are ready to sign the final contract. At this point the transfer of the title deed is completed, the balance of the money is paid and vacant possession given. The deed must then be registered at the Registry office.

Extra costs you will be responsible for will include: Land Registry fees, which are on a sliding scale depending on the value of the property but are usually around 7 per cent; stamp duty payable within 30 days of completion; fee for the application to the Council of Ministers; and your lawyer's fees, which will vary according to the amount of work he has carried out. Check at the outset whether or your not you are expected to pay the estate agent's fee. Home-buyers are advised to consider the implications of local inheritance and capital gains tax legislation and take advice on whether or not it would benefit them to draw up a Cypriot will.

If you are buying off-plan, it would be wise to have your lawyer check the agreement which should include details of specifications, payment, schedule of works and so on. Expect to have to make payments in stages which vary according to the individual developer. Make sure you hold back the final tranche until six months after completion in case there any glitches.

Useful Addresses

Cyprus High Commission
93 Park Street
London W1Y 4ET
Tel: 020 7499 8272

Cyprus Tourist Office
17 Hanover Street
London W1S 1YP
Tel: 020 7569 8800

Cyprus Trade Centre
Third Floor, 29 Princes Street
London W1R 7RG
Tel: 020 7629 6288

House-hunters

Above *Potamatissa is a small mountain village where Pam and Derek looked at a four-bedroomed hideaway.*

Pam and Derek Hardy

Tired of the dreary British weather, Pam and Derek Hardy were seeking a dream retirement home in the sun. They were looking for something with lots of space to accommodate their five grandchildren, preferably with a pool, but were otherwise quite open-minded about the possibilities. They had visited Cyprus 15 years earlier and felt it would suit them as a permanent home.

Páfos was the first place they visited, in response to an advertisement for a private sale in the local paper. The two-bedroomed Villa Pandora was an attractive bungalow done up in a very English style and on the market for £79,000. The *pièce de résistance* was the bar. This took up part of the new extension that opened on to the pool. Pam was impressed. 'It seemed so big and I liked the open-plan style. It would be a bit of a squeeze to fit our family in there all at once but we could just manage it. I can imagine having barbecues outside and we both really liked the bar.' That was a pity because the owners planned to take it with them. The other snag was that the extension was not on the deeds. The owner had been assured by the mayor that she didn't need planning permission; nonetheless she had agreed to pay for an architect to register the extension in order to put any prospective buyer's mind at ease. In the end they decided that although they liked the area, the property was ultimately too dark inside.

Next they went into the Troödos mountains to the little village of Potamatissa to see if they liked the idea of a mountain retreat and to see how much further their

money would go there than it would on the coast. The four-bedroomed house was built over two levels into a cliff with a price tag of £40,000. The most striking room was the open-plan living area with a large fireplace, high ceilings and whitewashed walls. The whole place was in good decorative order and commanded spectacular views across the valley. 'We thought it was most unusual. We loved the wooden walkways and big, open fireplace. In fact, it reminded us of a log cabin we once stayed in in New Zealand.' However, Derek was put off by the scary drive to the village. 'I'm not a nervous driver, but I could become one!'

In the appealing, perfectly preserved village of Lefkara, a recently renovated traditional stone house had an asking price of £63,000. It had two bedrooms and bathrooms, a large kitchen and a rooftop terrace with views to die for. It was a bit too small for Pam and Derek, although they were very positive about it. 'We liked the whole house though I think the spiral staircase might be a bit hairy for the children. If we bought it, we might put the bedrooms downstairs so we could live with those views. You'd never get tired of them.'

Last on the list was a three-bedroomed town villa in Larnaca. It was less than a year old and selling at the bargain price of £77,000. The architect, Amilcar Fernandez, showed Pam and Derek round, taking them through the two beautifully arranged sitting areas, the fitted kitchen, the luxury bathrooms and the large loft space. 'It was an absolutely beautiful place. You know it's going to be lovely before you go in but it's breathtaking inside.' Well designed, with furniture for which they could negotiate as part of the purchase, this looked like the perfect answer to Pam and Derek's search. But there was no swimming pool and they preferred the beaches at Páfos. Then, after serious reflection, they reluctantly decided the island was not for them after all.

'It's a long way to travel for our family and the island is small and you can't really go anywhere else. What we've decided to do instead is take a long let of at least six months in Spain. I think we'll probably end up living there almost permanently because of the weather. Our family can easily travel to us by train and car as well as plane. I want us to learn a bit of Spanish and live there so we know what it's like. Then the minute we see the right place, we'll buy it.'

'If we bought it, we might put the bedrooms downstairs so we could live with those views. You'd never get tired of them.'

Building, restoring, renovating

How many of us have fantasised about buying the ideal plot, the ruin with potential, the house that becomes the home of our dreams? These fantasies can be transformed into reality, but without the necessary research and care, they can only too easily turn into a nightmare. Unless you are fluent in the language of the country where you are moving, building, restoring or renovating abroad can be fraught with problems. You will need the help of an expert – probably an architect.

When buying a plot of land or property to restore, there are various considerations to bear in mind. Make sure planning permission has been granted to develop the site and check how much time you have before it expires. Check the likelihood of other developments in the neighbourhood that may affect your plans in terms of noise, neighbours or spoilt views. Conditions of the land that may affect the planning and cost of your build include sloping ground, the position of trees, ground conditions and access to mains connections for gas, electricity and water. If reaching your site is difficult, you will have to arrange access so that materials can be brought to it. Confirm that the boundaries of the site on the title deeds are

those that you believe you are being sold, and make sure that there are no public rights of way, covenants or easements on your land. Your solicitor should be able to advise you on all these matters.

Before buying an old property for restoration, you should have it checked by a surveyor so that you know exactly what you are letting yourself in for. In remote rural areas, it is unlikely to have a damp-proof course or to be connected to gas, electricity or water supplies, and it will frequently need new windows and doors. The roof may be falling in and, at the very least, you will almost certainly want to add all mod cons in the kitchen and bathroom. If there are outbuildings you are hoping to make habitable, they will need to be checked, too.

Historic buildings may be protected by a heritage organisation (the equivalent of our English Heritage), in which case you will have to conform with various regulations that may specify, for example, materials, exterior style and colours, and the number of floors. If you do not want to be restricted in this way, you will have no choice but to choose another property. It is also possible that you will not be able to extend your building beyond the footprint of the original, which may limit your plans. In any event, you should try to be sensitive to the area in which you're building and respect local traditions and styles so that your new home blends comfortably into the area. Permission for building a swimming pool is not always granted, so check before you buy. Whatever you do, do not embark on any work without the necessary planning permission, otherwise a local council will have the power to make you pull everything down.

If you can speak the language, have the necessary skills, time and the patience of Job, there is no reason why you shouldn't undertake the work yourself. However, if you have any worries about bodging something, bring in a professional. A fundamental mistake could prove extremely expensive if subsequently the place has to be pulled down to repair it. Be aware that there may be some work where you are legally obliged to employ a professional. For example, in France a fuse box must be installed by a qualified electrician. If you decide to ignore this and an accident occurs, you may find that the resulting damage is not covered by your insurance.

Most people will probably embark on the work using an architect and builders. You can bring in labour from outside the region but it may alienate the local professionals who you will doubtless need one day. If you cannot be on hand throughout the build, you will need to appoint a project manager or architect to oversee it. Bear in mind that it will inevitably take much longer than you expect. Working practices will not necessarily follow the pattern you are familiar with in the UK so it will be advantageous to have someone in charge who knows what to expect. Again, finding an architect should be done with the help of your estate agent, notary or other expatriates who have undertaken similar work. The same precautionary measures should be taken as with builders. Talk through the work you want done, listen to their advice and go through the resulting plans very carefully. Make sure you understand exactly what they will be responsible for, what and how you will pay them and if there are any restrictive clauses if the work goes over budget or time.

Craftsmen from the locality will be much better acquainted with local building practices, materials and where to get them. It is also cheaper to employ people from the area. The only way to find reliable builders is to talk to local people, take advice from your architect and get references from, or talk to, any builder's previous employers. If you can, go and look at other buildings for which they've been responsible so that you will be happy about the quality of their work. Ideally, with your architect, you should obtain three estimates for the work required. Be as specific as you can about every detail of the work involved. How much you spend depends on your requirements, but remember to monitor the costs carefully as the work progresses and to retain a contingency sum of at least 10 per cent of the total price in case things go wildly wrong. Confirm whether the fee quoted is fixed or an estimate, and whether the work comes with any guarantees after its completion.

Remember to keep all receipts during the build since you may be able offset them against rental costs or capital gains tax when you sell the property. Also, check how much of the original building needs to be kept if you are to avoid paying VAT.

Invest in one or two books that go into the subject in depth so you have a clear idea of how to avoid the pitfalls and derive the greatest satisfaction from fulfilling your dreams.

Unless you are fluent in the language of the country you are moving to, building abroad can be fraught with problems. You will need the help of an expert, probably an architect.

Building, restoring, renovating ....

Croatia

Croatia has many attractions: clear turquoise seas, ancient fishing villages, craggy castles, diverse national parks, and idyllic islands. Although memories of its recent history as a war zone may linger on, this country has now been at peace for some years and welcomes the return of foreign visitors. Croatia neatly divides into two distinct parts: the coastal and the continental regions. The coast is so craggy that although it is only about 600 kilometres long as the crow flies from north to south, it actually winds through 1,777 kilometres of inlets, coves, cliffs, headlands and beaches. Offshore, there are 1,185 islands – large and small, fertile and barren. As only a mere 66 of these are inhabited, the rest are a sailor's paradise.

Croatia has a diverse history. Its remains have been respected and preserved down the years, so that Roman ruins exist alongside medieval walled towns and elegant Venetian-style town houses. The Latin-based influence in the architecture and way of life on the coast is in stark contrast to inland, continental Croatia, where the atmosphere comes closer to its neighbours, Austria and Hungary. In many ways unspoiled and relaxed, this new-old nation might be the ideal place to find a bolthole away from it all.

Croatia lies in the southern part of central Europe, a C-shaped country bordered by the Adriatic coastline to the west, Slovenia and Hungary to the north, and Serbia and Bosnia-Herzegovina to the east and south. Like the other Balkan states, it has had a volatile history with numerous occupying powers, including the Romans, Venetians and Ottomans, as well as France and Austro-Hungary. In 1919, the Kingdom of the Slavs, Croats and Slovenes was established with Montenegro and Serbia. This hybrid state endured a number of troubled years until becoming part of the federated kingdom of Yugoslavia in 1929.

But Croatian nationalism lived on, surfacing during the Second World War, when the country was occupied by the Axis powers, and in sporadic risings against the re-established, but now communist, Yugoslavia in the post-war years. It was only in 1991, however, that Croatia was able to declare its independence. Immediately, the ethnic Serbs in the region of Krajina openly dissented. They were supported by the Yugoslav federal army and heavy fighting began. The UN peace-keeping forces were deployed and, in 1992, the EC recognised Croatia's independence. Within months the country was admitted into the UN, although fighting against the Serbs continued until 1995, when the Dayton Agreement was signed. This meant that Croatia's traditional borders, including the secessionist region of eastern Slavonia, were guaranteed.

Croatia's long popularity as a tourist destination was interrupted by these political disturbances but now, at last, it is able to welcome visitors once again. They are drawn to its fine coastline and myriad islands by the promise of warm summers and mild winters by the sea. The Dinaric Alps rise majestically behind the beaches in their isolated coves beyond the coastal plains, effectively dividing coastal from continental Croatia. The country's rich cultural history is evident everywhere. In particular, there is a wealth of Roman remains, ranging from the splendid ruined palace at Split, built by the Emperor Diocletian, to the amphitheatre at Pula. Everywhere there are elegant fortified towns and traditional fishing villages that frequently owe their style to the days of Venetian occupation. The coastal climate is Mediterranean but away from the sea the temperatures are cooler. Inland, the southern European flavour of the coast gives way to a more central European feel, perfectly expressed in the baroque architecture of Zagreb and other inland towns.

The large majority of the population is Roman Catholic and many of the festivals celebrated throughout the country are religious or based on Croatian folk traditions. Colourful local costumes are frequently worn and folk music and dancing are still popular throughout the country. Dances vary from a lively round dance to the more dramatic sword dances that are associated with the island of Korčula. Various crafts have developed over the years, but perhaps the best known is the Croatian embroidery that often features the red and white squares of the Croatian flag. The island of Pag is known for its lacemaking and still uses designs that have been passed down through the generations.

Croatian cuisine has inevitably been influenced by the many cultures involved in its history. Inland, the cooking displays its Hungarian, Viennese and Turkish origins. Popular dishes are mainly meat-based and include turkey, duck or goose with *mlinci* (doughballs), *gulaš* (Hungarian goulash) *čevapčici* (meat kebabs) and steak *à la Zagreb* (deep-fried breaded veal stuffed with ham and cheese).

On the coast, the food typically takes on a more Mediterranean flavour, with the emphasis on fresh fish and vegetables cooked simply with olive oil, herbs and garlic. It is not surprising that fish features widely here – reputedly, over 400 varieties are available, including gilt-headed bream, grouper, mackerel, sea bass, cuttlefish, sardines and langoustines. Risotto flavoured with squid, *menestra* (similar to minestrone), Dalmatian ham, *brodet* (fish stew) and *pasticada* (a rich beef stew) are all popular dishes. Specialities from the islands include *vitalac* (spit-roasted lamb offal in lamb gut)

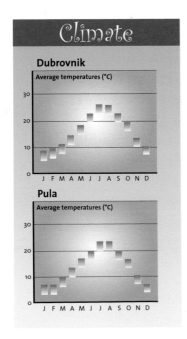

Climate

Dubrovnik
Average temperatures (°C)

Pula
Average temperatures (°C)

from Brač, spit-roasted pilchards from Vis and cheese from Pag. The Dalmatian region has produced many great wines since Roman times including Dingač, Postup, Kastellet and Malmsey from Dubrovnik. The islands have their own special vintages such as Vugava from Vis, Prc from Hvar, Grk and Pošip from Korčula, Marastina from Lastovo and Plavač from Brač, or you could try the local beers from Zagreb and Karlovač.

Most foreigners looking for a home in the Croatian sun look in Istria, along the Dalmatian coast or on the islands. Istria is the largest peninsula in the Adriatic and has always had strong links with Italy. Cut off from the rest of Croatia by the Dinaric Alps, and with borders that have changed a number of times over its history, Istria offers a cosmopolitan atmosphere charged with a dynamism that is lacking along the more relaxed Dalmatian coast. Most of the resort towns lie along the western coast of the peninsula, many of them displaying both Venetian and Austro-Hungarian influences in their architecture. The landscape here boasts pine forests, vineyards and olive groves dotted with old stone houses and windmills.

The capital of the region is Pula, which was chosen by the Romans as their base in the first century BC. Evidence of their presence is still seen in the organisation of the streets in the old quarter, the remains of the amphitheatre, the Triumphal Arch of Sergius and the ancient forum where remains of ancient buildings still stand. Now the centre of Istrian commercial life, Pula is where James Joyce briefly lived and taught when the Austro-Hungarian empire claimed the area around Trieste. It is an ideal starting point for visiting the Brijuni islands; once reserved for the use of the Communist dictator Marshal Tito and later Franjo Tudjman, they are now a national park.

Istria's most remarkable town of all must be Rovinj, a fishing port known as the Venus of Mediterranean architecture. The old town is completely contained in an oval peninsula which looks south across the harbour and east towards the surrounding wooded hills. It is dominated by the baroque hilltop Cathedral of St Euphemia. Once an island, the channel separating Rovinj from the mainland was filled in during the 18th century, allowing the town to spread.

Poreč is the is the centre of the region's tourism, offering a wild range of day- and night-time entertainment. As elsewhere, the Romans have left their legacy in the street layout and names, although the elegant stone buildings are Venetian in origin. The pride of Poreč is the sixth-century Euphrasian Basilica, a World Heritage site boasting some of the world's finest Byzantine art. To the north and south of the town, the coastline bristles with tourist resorts. The undulating hinterland bears comparison to Tuscany, and peace and quiet characterise the historic hill towns.

Until war broke out in 1991, the Dalmatian coast was a magnet for holidaymakers. As people begin to visit the country again, they find it unspoilt and uncrowded, offering a wide choice of beautiful places to get away from it all.

Split is situated on a peninsula and built around a sheltered harbour. It is the largest city in central Dalmatia. The old town lies within the walls of Diocletian's Palace, built 1,700 years ago. Here Diocletian, the scourge of Christians, lived until his

Facts

Capital Zagreb
Population 4,282,000
Land area 56,538 sq km
Currency 1 Croatian kuna (HRK) = 100 lipas
Electricity 220v
Time zone GMT + 1 hour
Religion Predominantly Roman Catholic
Language Croatian
Government Presidential/parliamentary democracy

Below Round Rovinj's cathedral wind narrow cobbled streets, red-tiled stone houses with their unique exterior chimneys and small squares – all built in a bewildering variety of styles.

Above South of Split, Makarska is a cosmopolitan resort offering the best of both worlds, old and new.

Below Dubrovnik suffered badly during the recent war, but restoration work to the buildings, particularly to the tiled roofs, has been carefully carried out.

death in 313. In the seventh century, the inhabitants of nearby Salona (Solin) were driven from their town by the Avars and Slavs and sought refuge within the palace walls. They built their homes inside the seven-acre compound, incorporating the original Roman remains into their architecture. Today the old town is a place of white stone buildings, bustling with shops, cafés and restaurants and home to Split's most important historic and cultural buildings. Beside the northern entrance to the palace stands the huge statue of Grgur Ninski, a ninth-century bishop, whose gleaming big toe testifies to the number of passers-by touching it to have their wishes granted. Split is a thriving port and university town with plenty of attractions, including a number of museums and churches, the National Theatre, various archaeological sites and a sulphur spa right next to the indoor fish market. The town is also enlivened by various annual festivals including the February Carnival, the Split Summer Festival and the Festival of Popular Music, which is held in June.

Between Split and Dubrovnik there are a number of charming old walled towns, tourist resorts sheltered by pine forests, small villages huddled at the foot of the mountains and captivating beaches. Finally, Dubrovnik itself. The playwright George Bernard Shaw said, 'Those who seek paradise on Earth should come to Dubrovnik and see Dubrovnik.' Once a trading port that rivalled Venice, it is regarded as one of the best preserved medieval towns in the world despite an earthquake in 1667 destroying most of the Renaissance architecture with the exception of the Rector's Palace and Sponza Palace.

The old city is surrounded by its original walls which protect narrow cobbled streets, open marble-paved squares, uniform tall white houses, monasteries, churches and tourist attractions such as the aquarium. It is effectively divided by the Placa, a wide, marble, paved street lined with café terraces and shops. Formerly a shallow marine channel dividing an island from the mainland, it once represented a social divide in the city. The nobles lived on what used to be the island, whereas the poorer people inhabited the steep streets that climb up to the northern city walls. Cutting through them at right angles is Prijeko, one of the most popular areas for eating out. To the north-west of the old town, the wooded Lapad peninsula has been developed into a pleasant residential area. Other good places to look for property extend to Trsteno in the north and Cavtat in the south.

The Dubrovnik Riviera has a number of attractive small towns such as Cavtat and Mlini. Cavtat is an elegant resort centred on a natural harbour and surrounded by fertile hills. The lively, palm-lined promenade round the harbour, with its pavement cafés and restaurants, is the centre of activity. However, the town also has a history dating back to Greek and Roman times. There are interesting buildings such as the Renaissance Rector's Palace; the Baroque parish church; local art gallery; and a Franciscan monastery close to the domed mausoleum, which was designed by the sculptor, Meštrović.

Out of town, along the coast, there are tourist developments that enjoy the warm, clear seas and offer every watersport under the sun. Mlini is a picture-perfect fishing village that is named after the watermill in its centre. Sitting at the foot of high mountains, it enjoys the protection of pine woods, citrus and olive groves. Its old stone houses lead down to the harbour and pretty shoreline. Only a short drive away is the Zupa valley, which is dotted with old farmhouses, traditional villages and vineyards, the botanical gardens at Trsteno, and the wildlife of the Neretva Delta and the Konavle Valley. This is an area free of the tourist developments that have sprung up further north, an area where tranquillity, a relaxed pace of life, peace and quiet can be guaranteed.

Perhaps the most special aspect of coastal Croatia is the multiplicity of islands only a short boat ride away. Each has its own traditions and characteristics and offers an idyllic holiday hideaway.

Brač, just off the coast from Makarska and Split, is one of the largest islands in the Adriatic. It is famous for its white stone, which has been used in construction all over the world, from Diocletian's Palace in Split to the White House in Washington. The indented coast provides plenty of secluded bays, but the most popular beach of all must be the Zlatni Rat, or Golden Horn, a long spit of sand that extends into the sea at Bol and changes shape with the wind and the waves. Bol is one of the two resort towns on the island and nowadays is Croatia's windsurfing centre. The town itself was once a medieval sea port and its charm has been retained thanks to the practice of building hotels in the pine forests outside. Its cultural attractions include a Dominican monastery and a Renaissance palace where exhibitions of modern Croatian art are held. Other resort towns are on the north of the island, the largest of which is Supetar, and there are a number of sleepy fishing villages close to almost deserted beaches. Inland, the island is green and wooded. The stony ground has been cleared over the centuries to make orchards, olive groves and vineyards.

Below *The picturesque fishing village of Milna, on the island of Brač, has not been spoilt by tourist development.*

Hvar is known for both its wines and its lavender, the smell of which scents the island for much of the year. It also enjoys the reputation of being the sunniest island in Croatia – hence its claim to the title of the Croatian Riviera. There are a number of resorts and unspoilt villages in matchless rural settings. The island is rich in history – the old town of Stari Grad was founded in 385 BC by the Greeks. Surrounded by woods on a 6-kilometre long bay, the majority of buildings date back to the 16th and 17th centuries, though evidence of earlier cultures can still be seen.

Hvar town is the largest and most stylish on the island. A palm-lined promenade runs along the coast and the traffic-free marble streets present exquisitely carved house fronts. The principal attractions of Hvar include the polished main square, Trg Sveti Stjepana; the Arsenal; the old municipal theatre; a Venetian palace; and the spectacular Cathedral of St Stjepan. Along the indented coastline lies a string of modest, easy-going towns such as Vrboska and Jelsa. Both are built on narrow inlets with Renaissance and Baroque buildings surrounding the central squares, while a variety of villas hide in the surrounding pine woods.

Korčula is one of the greenest islands, renowned for its cork oak forests that traditionally supplied the shipbuilding industry. It has a lush, fertile interior where small villages lie among vineyards and olive groves. The island was first settled by the Greeks and has a fascinating history that is displayed in some of its traditions. The most famous is the Moreska Sword Dance, which re-enacts the battles against the Moors. It is performed by the people of Korčula town throughout July and August. Other sword dances, the *kumpanjinja* and *mostra*, are popular elsewhere in the island. Korčula town is supposedly the birthplace of Marco Polo. The old town is built on a peninsula and resembles a miniature Dubrovnik. It is a small walled area with a herringbone pattern of streets. The central square is dominated by the Cathedral of St Mark, which took the community 150 years to complete. There are many attractive small townships on the island such as Zrnovo, with its old stone houses and bell towers, Racisce, Pupnat, Lumbarda and Cara. Any of these could be of an idyllic place in the sun.

Although most holiday homebuyers will head for the coast, the attractions of continental Croatia should not be forgotten. At its heart is the city of Zagreb, a stately city reminiscent of Vienna or Budapest. The centre of the town is divided between the upper and lower town, Gornje Grad and Donji Grad; the medieval streets of the former contrast with the 19th-century elegance of the latter. Highlights of the city include the main square, Trg Jelacica, the churches of St Catherine and St Mark, and a number of first-rate museums and art galleries. Outside the city, there are fortified castles, monasteries and unspoilt traditional towns that offer a real escape from the hustle and bustle of contemporary life.

House prices and the cost of living in Croatia are low. The spectacular country and coastline are unexploited and remain one of the best-kept secrets in Europe.

Above The 13th-century city walls of Hvar town enclose marble streets, narrow alleyways and a wealth of historic residential buildings.

How to get there

Air
British Airways fly from Gatwick to Zagreb. Croatian Airways fly from Heathrow and Gatwick to Pula, Zagreb, Split and Dubrovnik.
Flight time: 2 hours

A Place in the Sun

How to buy property in...
Croatia

Estate agency in Croatia is in its comparative infancy, particularly along the Dalmatian coast. It is worth supplementing your search by visiting local shops and bars to learn about properties that may not be registered with estate agents in the main towns yet may be for sale. Having found your property, it's essential to find a bilingual lawyer who will be able to guide you through the buying process so you avoid any expensive mistakes. The local embassy should be able to help you.

Your lawyer will draw up a contract which will include all the relevant details of the buyer, seller and the property, including the agreed price. It should also include any conditional clauses that may enable the buyer to withdraw from the deal if they are not fulfilled. It will specify all costs and taxes that will be due as a result of the purchase, as well as the date and any other conditions relevant to completion.

At this point a deposit of 10–15 per cent of the purchase price is paid. If the buyer does not complete the purchase within the specified time, he loses the deposit. If the seller sells the property to someone else during that time, he must pay the buyer a sum twice that of the deposit. The final contract must be drawn up by the lawyer and witnessed by a notary. The lawyer must apply to the Ministry of Law and the Ministry for Foreign Affairs on the buyer's behalf for an Act of Permission. If the buyer owns a company in Croatia, this application is not necessary. The transaction is recorded in the Land Registry but it is only officially registered when the Act of Permission has been granted.

Hidden costs include a 5 per cent purchase tax that is based on the value of the property as estimated by the Ministry of Finance; lawyer's and notary's fees that will amount to a further 2 per cent; estate agent's fees of 3.5 per cent if you have used one. Other on-going costs will include the annual payment of a non-resident's tax ($£1/m^2$ per year) and land tax.

As with buying in any other country, make sure you check any implications there may be from Croatian inheritance laws and take the right precautions to protect yourself in the future.

Useful Addresses

Croatian Embassy and Consulate General
21 Conway Street
London W1T 6BN
Tel: 020 7387 1790 (embassy)
Tel: 020 7387 1144 (consulate)

Croatian National Tourist Office
2 Lanchesters
162–164 Fulham Palace Road
London W6 9ER
Tel: 020 8563 7979

House-hunters

Monika Stedul and James Fergusson

Monika and James met while working for the international peace-keeping force in Sarajevo after the Balkan war. Monika is half-Croatian and, although they moved back to work as consultants in London, their love affair with Croatia's Dalmatian coast, which began when they holidayed there from Bosnia, continued.

Above Monika and James welcomed the prospect of restoring an old property such as this one on Hvar.

'The Adriatic Sea is as clean as anywhere in the world. It's got everything the Mediterranean has to offer – great climate, great seafood. But the prices are a quarter of what they would be in western Europe.'

When they returned to look for a second home, they wanted to find somewhere that they could buy and restore within their budget of £50,000. Their only other requirement was that the property had a view. Having searched on the coast, they went to the island of Hvar, a two-hour ferry ride from the ancient Roman port town of Split. Inland, they looked at a 130-year-old two-bedroomed stone house on the market for £11,000. With no electricity or running water, the conditions were basic but the living room, bedrooms and two cellar rooms had the potential to be turned into something very special. 'It's a fantastic project, although difficult to do if we're based in the UK.' A local builder quoted a price of £30,000 for the entire restoration works and promised e-mails including three-dimensional images to keep them posted on progress. But Monika and James were nervous that the work might not end up in the traditional style they wanted. 'It's a great opportunity and tempting because it's so cheap, but it's too hemmed in in the village.'

In the south of the island, they saw a two-bedroomed clifftop house on the market for £46,000. Built in the 1980s, it was on three levels and had a terrace on each with a view right out to sea. 'It's not what we were looking for in terms of architecture but it definitely has potential. There's lots of outside space which would be great, and the unfinished top-floor room could be a study or extra bedroom.' Although encouraged by the information that the road connecting the area to Hvar town was being improved and that the owner might entertain an offer of 5 per cent to 15 per cent under the asking price, Monika and James decided to go on looking.

In the inland agricultural village of Dol, they saw a traditional village home which sprawled over three main buildings surrounding a central courtyard. The original house had a cellar and attic and still contained the typical Croatian living room and three bedrooms, although the kitchen was now used for storage. Instead,

> **'It's so different from what we had in mind but it certainly has the "wow" factor in terms of location.'**

A Place in the Sun

the newest building held the kitchen and dining room. This had been built in the 1970s without planning permission, so was not covered by the government's amnesty on buildings built without permission before 1969, although a lawyer didn't think it would be be a problem. 'It's like walking into a museum. Being so higgledy piggledy and on so many levels gives it great charm. It does need work and we'd love to open it up a bit. But... the separate parts don't add up to a whole with that magic that you need.'

Finally Monika and James took the ferry over to Korčula where they viewed a stunning four-bedroomed villa built right on the coast with three terraces, a garage and beach access. It was divided into a couple of two-bedroomed flats and a studio, all with breathtaking unobstructed views out to sea. 'It's so different from what we had in mind but it certainly has the "wow" factor in terms of location.'

Although none of these four properties quite matched what the couple were looking for, they returned home having made up their mind that they wanted to be in Hvar and plan to return as soon as they can to stake out more property in their painstaking search for the perfect holiday home.

Above *The Korčula villa put a new angle on Monica and James's house hunting. They thought it was fantastic and was quite unlike anything they had imagined themselves buying.*

Left *The villa was so close to the sea that the wonderful views will never be obstructed.* ·

Leaving it all behind

Whether you are moving permanently or only plan to spend a chunk of the year in your new home, there will be numerous ends to tie up before you go.

If you have sold up and are moving permanently, you should make a checklist of the people and organisations that you will need to notify of your move and change of address. These will include your bank, solicitor, accountant, Inland Revenue, insurance companies, credit card companies, hire purchase companies, rental companies, savings accounts and any local businesses with whom you may have accounts, such as department stores, newsagents and garages.

* Notify any company in whom you hold stocks and shares.
* Inform the DSS of your move regarding your benefits, allowances and pension.
* Cancel any club/society memberships and magazine subscriptions.
* Notify your dentist, optician, doctor and any other practitioner with whom you are registered. You may want to arrange for your medical and dental records to be forwarded or you could keep them yourself until you find a new doctor and dentist abroad. If you have health insurance, you should advise the company of your move and discuss any alternative arrangements you may need to make for you and your family.
* Cancel all insurance policies that will no longer be relevant such as those for kitchen appliances or your car. You may be liable to a refund.
* If you are proposing to drive abroad, check what you need to do about your licence. You may need to obtain an international driving licence from the AA or RAC. If so, it needs to be done before you leave the country. You may need to get a local licence for the country you are moving to. If so, check how to get one.
* Let the companies holding any life insurance policies know of your move.
* Give the mains suppliers (gas/water/electricity) and telephone company at least 48 hours' notice of your departure date and your new address so they can prepare your final accounts.
* Send out your change of address to all your friends and acquaintances and arrange with the post office to have all your mail forwarded.
* Arrange for any outstanding debts to be settled.
* If your children are at school, try to give a reasonable amount of notice of their departure. Notify any other clubs or classes that they many belong to.
* Finally, cancel your milk, find homes for your pot plants and return your library books.

If you are only leaving the country for a few months, you obviously will not have to see to all these things. Your principal concern will probably be your empty house. If you are only going to be away for a short time, you may prefer to leave it unoccupied. Make sure that you have a good burglar alarm and adequate insurance cover. Leave the key with an obliging neighbour in case of an emergency, cancel all deliveries and notify the local police of your absence. It's also an idea to get someone to look after the garden so that it doesn't betray the fact that its owner is away. There are agencies which provide house-sitters to look after your house, pets, plants and garden, which you may prefer as an alternative.

However, if you are going to be away for several months, you may prefer the security of knowing that your house is occupied and being looked after. If you don't have an obliging relative or friend to move in, you can employ an agency to handle the let for you. You will need to choose a reliable estate agent who also specialises in property management and is familiar with the legal and financial aspects of this side of the property market. Care does need to be taken in choosing the right tenancy agreement for your needs. It is well worth seeking the additional advice of your solicitor, who will explain the implications of the different options. Satisfy yourself that the agent will not only look after the letting of the house for you but also oversee the necessary maintenance. It can be difficult to know how much rental you should be charging for your home but listen to the advice of your estate agent and investigate for yourself to see what other similar properties fetch in your area.

When an agreement is drawn up between you and the letting agent, ask your solicitor to check it for you. Making sure every eventuality is covered, including your responsibilities, the agent's responsibilities, the tenant's responsibilities, any restrictions you particularly want to impose on the tenants, conditions of the termination of the lease and so on. You should also check that your furniture and gas appliances comply with the government's safety regulations.

If you are renting your property while you are abroad, it is essential that you check the terms of your insurance policy. You should let your insurers know that you are letting the house and confirm that the contents are fully insured in your absence. You will need to make a complete inventory both for your own peace of mind as well as theirs. If that is too arduous a job for you to undertake, your agent should be able to recommend a specialist firm who will do it for you. If you are leaving anything particularly valuable (not always a good idea), it can be worth making a photographic record. It may be preferable to put anything of real value in storage. You must also let your mortgage company know if you will be out of the country for some time.

When renting your house, it's vital you take into account everything that might go wrong – then it most probably won't. Therefore, it is imperative you seek professional advice on all aspects. An experienced estate agent, a solicitor and an accountant to explain any tax implications should cover all eventualities. It is best to travel abroad safe in the knowledge that when you return everything at home will be just as you left it.

Make a checklist of the people and organisations that you will need to notify of your move and change of address.

Bulgaria and Romania

Following the collapse of Communism in Eastern Europe from 1989, Bulgaria and Romania have recently been opening their doors to tourism once again.

Bulgaria is a beautiful and diverse country with a distinctive cultural heritage and an imposing topography. Its untouched forests and rural landscape are unrivalled in Europe. Although their history has been turbulent and often tragic, Bulgarians have a resilience and a capacity for celebration, hospitality and fun. With fine mountains, wonderful beaches and charming old villages and towns, they have every right to look to the future with optimism and determination.

Romania is a country of numerous delights and surprises. Its central and northern mountain landscapes give way to vine- and orchard-clad hills and plateaux. These, in turn, develop into fertile eastern agricultural plains that lead to the Black Sea Riviera. The choice of activities is extensive – whether skiing in traditional or modern resorts, hiking through unspoilt countryside, lazing on a beach, boating or studying the rich bird life in the Danube delta. Traditional villages, medieval castles, monasteries harbouring 16th-century artistic treasures, and a wealth of fascinating architecture, museums and galleries all await. This is a country ripe for exploration.

Facts: Bulgaria

Capital Sofia
Population 7,797,000
Land area 110,910 sq km
Currency 1 lev (Lv) = 100 stotinki
Electricity 220v
Time zone GMT + 2 hours
Religion Predominantly
Bulgarian Orthodox
Language Bulgarian
Government Parliamentary
democracy

Bulgaria may be at the eastern part of the Balkan peninsula, but for a British homebuyer it has a more Mediterranean feel. Bordered by Romania, Macedonia, Yugoslavia, Greece, Turkey and the Black Sea, it stands at the crossroads between Europe and Asia, northern Europe and the Mediterranean. Its history has often been one of violence. The first Bulgarian Empire was founded in 681 AD by the Bulgars, who were swiftly assimilated by the Slavs. 1362 saw the beginning of 500 years of Ottoman Turkish rule, although during this period, the Bulgarians took care to preserve the language and culture. A bloody revolution against the Turks began in 1876 but it wasn't until 1908 that Bulgaria was able to declare its full independence. In the 20th century Bulgaria was successively a kingdom, a communist state and (since 1989) an elective democracy. At the time of writing, the party of the monarch-in-exile, who was expelled by the Communists at the age of nine, had just been swept to power with a resounding majority.

After the fall of Communism, the Bulgarian people endured considerable hardship, poverty, corruption and inflation as their economy struggled to adjust to the free market. However, in the last five years, the government has turned this around by undertaking strict measures to stabilise the economy and the currency – the leva is now linked to the Deutschmark – and reduce inflation. They have begun negotiations for membership of both the EU and NATO. This has resulted in hardship for many people and, as a result, wages and prices are among the lowest in Europe. At the turn of the 21st century, this adjustment is still not complete and the standard of living remains persistently low.

The country may be in a state of transition but it still has plenty to offer the visitor. The magnificent Rila, Pirin, Rodopi, Balkan and Sredna Gora mountain ranges provide an ideal environment for a rich plant life and many wild animals and birds. There are great walking and climbing opportunities, although the areas are not always well mapped. However, they benefit from being without the crowds of tourists that are associated with well-trekked walking areas in the west. Popular winter resorts provide good skiing facilities. Hidden away in the highlands are plenty of traditional villages, monasteries and a number of stunning national parks.

For a change of pace, however, the towns of Sofia, Plovdiv and Veliko Tŭrnovo are the three main cultural centres of the country, all worth visiting for their museums and galleries. The Danube towns in the north have their own attractions, especially Ruse, with its historic centre, built in the style of an Austro-Hungarian border town, and its collection of beautiful buildings and city squares. The Black Sea coast, with its temperate climate and western-style tourist facilities, tends to hold most attractions for foreign house-hunters.

The Bulgarians are proud of their traditions and culture and have worked hard to preserve them. On 1 March every year, *martenitsa* (red and white

Above In the Pirin mountains, the village of Melnik was once a thriving town. Its former prosperity is reflected in its impressive houses.

ribbons) are worn by everyone to mark the beginning of spring and there are numerous folklore festivals that take place throughout the country all year round. The autonomous Bulgarian Orthodox church survived the years of Communism and guards its own traditions, though it remains part of the wider Orthodox communion, with worship conducted in the Byzantine rite. As for local crafts, embroidery, pottery, wood carving (secular and religious), and copper-working all retain their place in today's culture.

Bulgarian cuisine is rich in freshly grown vegetables – especially beans – and fruit. Specialities often rely on slow-baking in earthenware pots, such as *kavarma* (meat and vegetables in an earthenware dish), or meat may be grilled or spit roasted. Fish is available along the coast and by lakes and reservoirs, so watch out for *skumriya* (mackerel), either grilled or baked, and the occasional mountain trout. Bulgarian yoghurt has claims to be the finest in the world. The country is a large wine producer, with its wines becoming increasingly well known – Gumza, Dimiat, Mavrud, Melnik and Pamid are among them. There are also plenty of local spirits which are cheap and strong. They may be drunk diluted with water, in the case of *mastika* (similar to *anise* or *ouzo*), or, as with *slivova*, a fiery liqueur brandy made from plums, downed in one. There are also several kinds of locally brewed beer.

The Black Sea coast is the most popular starting point for British buyers searching for a cheap place in the sun, although for those expatriates already living in Bulgaria, its charms are matched by living in the mountains or in Sofia. It is more expensive buying property on the coast than inland, with the exception of Sofia. A traditional farmhouse could cost as little as 20 per cent of the price of a seaside villa. However, legislation covering foreigners buying homes is complex so make sure any property is legally available to you. Selling property to foreigners is a relatively new business in Bulgaria, so do not expect the same sort of service from estate agents that you find in the UK.

For expatriates living in Bulgaria, there are three options used by buyers. The first – marrying a Bulgarian – and the second – getting permission from the Ministry of Finance – are not really options for most people. The third options is to set up a company, which then becomes the owner of the property. These complexities may put off some, but the lack of foreign buyers is the reason why prices are one-fifth of those found in Spain – yet the summer weather is just as favourable and the cost of living lower. The government is said to be considering a law to make it easier for foreigners to buy.

All along the coastline are beautiful sandy and pebbly beaches that bask in hot temperatures during the summer but endure freezing conditions in the winter. The principal location is Varna, Bulgaria's main sea port. Founded in 585 BC by the Ancient Greeks, it has flourished as a trading centre ever since. Surrounded by hills, it is a town of character that is alive in summer with restaurants and bars, especially around its central square.

Below Nesebâr is famed for its 19th-century wooden houses, which are among the finest of their kind to be found along the Bulgarian coast.

A new scheme, 'Beautiful Bulgaria', has been responsible for the renovation of a large number of buildings in the town. The scheme is an international project funded by the EU and the UN to improve the city and raise its standards to those of the West. Worth investigating for property are the town's north-western suburbs where wealthy Bulgarians have built holiday homes and villas.

North of Varna, past the package-tour paradise of Golden Sands, there are villages where the authentic flavour of Bulgaria can still be found. Kranevo, Kavarna, Zlatni Piasatzi and Krapets are some of the places worth visiting on the coast. Inland, there are quiet communities such as Shabla and Durankulak. The rural landscape of Bulgaria provides a glimpse of a bygone age. Horses and carts are the common form of transport and farmers plough fields without the modern machinery so familiar to us. A favourite town is Balchik, whose unique skyline is composed of the red-tiled, whitewashed houses that line the steep cobbled streets. Various purpose-built beach resorts of varying appeal have been created all along the coast. They range from the largest resorts of Golden Sands and Sunny Beach to the more upmarket Albena, with its bars, restaurants and discos, and holiday villages such as Elenite or Rusalka.

Between Varna and the family resort of Sunny Beach further south, the villages are more depressed, suffering from the decrease in visitors from the Eastern bloc who holidayed here in numbers during the 1970s

and 1980s. A few kilometres south of Sunny Beach, a narrow isthmus joins the mainland with Nesebâr. It was formerly known as Mesembria, and was a Greek town that came into its own in Byzantine times. At one time there were as many as 40 churches and chapels built here by Byzantine noblemen. Now the locals rely on fishing and tourism for their livelihood, but some of the churches are still standing, as are some fine examples of 19th-century wooden architecture. The town is alive with galleries, museums, restaurants and souvenir shops. Back on the mainland, the town of Burgas has a seedy reputation but maintains a relaxed atmosphere with many shops, restaurants, cafés and an annual folk festival. Beyond Sozopol, with its attractive 19th-century houses, busy promenade and excellent beaches, lie some of the best beaches in Bulgaria.

Romania

Romania lies between the River Danube to the south and the former Soviet Republic of Moldova to the north. With a serene Black Sea coast, the dramatic, forested mountains of the Transylvanian Alps, vast plains – among the most fertile in Europe – and its access to the great Danube waterway, Romania is a beautiful and potentially wealthy country of over 22 million people, of whom about 8 per cent are ethnic Hungarians.

Yet for all its physical beauty, Romania's history has been scarred by centuries of conflict. Its early heyday under the Dacians ended with their conquest by the Romans in 106 AD. During the Middle Ages, the principalities of Muntenia, Moldavia and Transylvania endured constant intimidation from the Ottoman, Hungarian and Hapsburg Empires, although Transylvania was the only one to fall under the rule of all three. The Ottomans presented the biggest threat and were eventually seen off by a succession of princes: Mircea the Old, Vlad the Impaler, Michael the Brave and Constantin Brâncoveanu. It wasn't until 1918 that the three provinces were finally united as a kingdom.

However, in 1945, the Russians deposed King Michael and imposed a Communist regime which culminated in Nicolae Ceauşescu's notorious dictatorship. Finally, in 1989, after revolution had spread from Timisoara to the capital, Bucharest, Ceausescu and his wife were executed and the way was cleared for the newly democratic state of Romania. The process of reconstruction has been painful. At one point inflation rose above 300 per cent, while at its worst unemployment affected one Romanian in ten. Millions live in poverty as a result of the long and increasingly ruinous Ceauşescu years.

Although still struggling to recover from the brutality of previous regimes, the country has realised that it has much to offer foreign visitors and is encouraging tourists from western Europe. The landscape of Romania is enormously varied and beautiful. While the major towns are finding their way to the 21st century, there are parts of the countryside where the horse and cart is as common a method of transport as the car. The generous, hospitable people are proud of the traditions and customs which have been passed down through generations. The Romanian language is a legacy from Roman times. It uses the western alphabet and is more akin to Italian than to the Slavonic tongues spoken in the surrounding countries. This makes it considerably easier for western Europeans to learn.

Romanian cuisine is fresh country fare. A guest might be welcomed with a *ţuică* (a fierce plum brandy), which is the national drink, or a glass of local wine, served with bread and salt. This could be followed with *ciorbă* (soured soup of many varieties such as tripe, meatballs or vegetable), *sărmălute* (soured cabbage or vine leaves stuffed with meat, rice and herbs), *tochitură* (meat stews) *mititei* (grilled meat rolls with garlic served with mustard) and, best known, *mămăligă* (polenta with yoghurt or sour cream). Desserts range through sweet cheese pastries to doughnuts or pancakes. To wash down your meal, there are local beers or, best of all, a range of Romanian wines of which the most well known are Grasa de Cotnari, Tamaioasa, Murfatlar, Târnave and Stefanesti.

Foreigners looking for a home here are most likely to be attracted to the areas of

Transylvania or the Black Sea Riviera, which tend to be more western in feel. Transylvania is probably the most straightforward place to buy because although property was previously state-owned, the people now have deeds to their property, which is not always the case elsewhere. If you are not moving to work or to return to your roots, buying property here is for the adventurous at heart or for those with an eye on investment. Since 1989, rapid privatisation and the diminishing role of the government in the real-estate area has meant property has boomed. The UNAI (National Union of Estate Agents) has been established to protect buyers from being exploited by inexperienced, self-styled estate agents. All reputable estate agents are registered with them.

Thanks to Hollywood and Bram Stoker, Transylvania conjures up visions of dark woods, gothic castles, howling werewolves and vampires, and, most fearsome of all, Dracula. But be unafraid, be very unafraid. Transylvania is a place of exceptional beauty with dramatic forested scenery, gothic castles, alpine meadows, medieval towns and unspoilt rural villages with enchanting churches and painted monasteries. In the summer, walkers can enjoy some of the best hiking Romania has to offer; in the winter, there are plenty of skiing opportunities.

Medieval Saxons migrating from their northern homeland founded the picturesque town of Braşov in the 12th century. According to legend, the children spirited away by the Pied Piper of Hamelin ended up near Braşov's main square, Piaţa Sfatului. Overlooking the town is Cetatea Braşov, an old citadel now converted to house a couple of bars, a restaurant and disco. The town has plenty of other cafés and restaurants, particularly around Piaţa Sfatului – the ideal spot for people-watching. There are houses (in need of extensive renovation) to be found for sale in the old town. These are certainly preferable to the utilitarian housing, once built for incoming Moldavian workers, situated on the outskirts of the town.

The countryside around Braşov is green and wooded. To the south-west, nestling at the foot of Mount Postavaru (with an altitude of 1,800 metres), is Poiana Braşov, Romania's most popular ski resort. It boasts a number of ski runs and slalom courses with a season that lasts from December to March. Other winter sports centres in the area include: Predeal, another thriving resort, which is both the highest-altitude Romanian ski resort and the starting point for some exciting summer hiking; Buşteni; and Sinaia, which is known as 'the Pearl of the Carpathians' thanks to its spectacular scenery. If you are a keen skier looking for a base nearby, there are flats for sale in the resorts and new wooden chalets are being built.

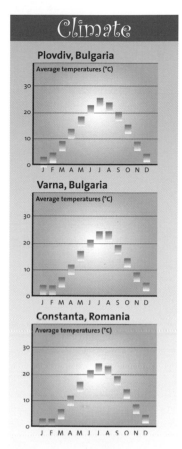

Climate

Plovdiv, Bulgaria
Average temperatures (°C)

Varna, Bulgaria
Average temperatures (°C)

Constanta, Romania
Average temperatures (°C)

Left Braşov's main square is lined with red-tiled and painted merchants' houses that surround the sturdy Council House.

Above Thanks to the legend of Dracula, Bran is the best-known village in Transylvania.

One town not to be missed is Bran, famous as the home of Dracula and complete with a castle that lives up to Stoker's story. But exploring Transylvania yields up many unspoilt medieval villages such as Sighisoara, with its UNESCO-protected historical centre; Sibiu; Hărman; Prejmer; Năsăud and Bistriţa, which is famed as the setting for Dracula. However, life in the remoter reaches of the country would be more difficult for an expatriate as the infrastructure is poor and utilities unreliable.

The country's capital, Bucharest, is situated between the Carpathian foothills and the Danube. According to legend, it was founded by a shepherd called Bucur. After Romania gained independence, the city was remodelled in the style of Paris, with long, wide boulevards and distinctively grand architecture. During the 1930s, it was known as 'little Paris' and the standard of living was as high as anywhere in the West. Much of the historical centre was demolished under Ceauşescu and replaced with monolithic concrete buildings, most notably the Palace of Parliament, which claims to be the second largest building in the world and was nicknamed Casa Nebunului (madman's house). However, the city still boasts plenty of green, open spaces, a number of historic churches and museums, and various architectural monuments. It also has plenty of restaurants and an animated night life.

The Black Sea Riviera is enormously popular during the summer when it basks in dry, mild weather. Constanţa is now Romania's second biggest city and largest port. The city's laid-back atmosphere is livened up by a cultural life that includes cinemas, a theatre, an opera house and plenty of restaurants and bars. To the north is the popular seaside resort of Mamaia, ideal for swimming and idling in the sun. Watersports are available there and at nearby Lake Siutghiol. Other resorts have been developed up and down the coast: Cosinesti, a lively place offering a wide variety of entertainment and favoured by the young; Eforie Nord and Mangalia, two of Romania's several health spas; and Neptun and Olimp, both more upmarket resorts on the edge of the Comorova forest, offering artificial lakes, sports facilities, a cinema and theatre, and shopping. North of the beaches lies the Danube Delta whose flood plain is a paradise for animals and birds. In 1990, the region was declared a Biosphere Reserve with a number of protected zones. The 'Threshold to the Delta' is Tulcea, a town first established by the Greeks as a port. Its main attractions are the Museum of the Danube Delta, the Art Museum and the ancient ruins of Aegyssus. The Delta is dotted with small towns and villages could be useful bases from which to explore the rest of the area.

Romania and Bulgaria may not seem the most obvious choice for your place in the sun, but if you have time to explore and have an eye for an investment, they may be the answer to your dreams.

How to get there

Air
British Airways fly from Gatwick to Sofia. Balkan Bulgarian Airlines fly from Heathrow to Sofia. Balkan Holidays operate charter flights in the summer from 10 UK air ports to Varna and Bourgas. In the winter they operate charter flights from Gatwick and Manchester to Plovdiv and Sofia. TAROM fly directly from Heathrow to Bucharest. British Airways fly directly from Gatwick to Bucharest.
Flight time: 3½–4½ hours

A Place in the Sun

How to buy property in...
Bulgaria & Romania

Bulgaria

At the time of writing, foreigners can buy a property in Bulgaria but not the land on which it is built, although they may buy limited rights such as right of use. There are also strict zoning restrictions which must be observed. To buy land, you must establish a company in Bulgaria. However, legislation is changing all the time, so you will need a good solicitor who understands the exact state of play and will guide you correctly through the process. The best solicitors may not always speak English, so a good interpreter is vital.

A notary draws up the the purchase contract in the form of a notary deed. He will need certain documents which provide proof that you are buying an unencumbered property and that you have the funds to do so. They will include one certifying the ownership right of the seller; a certificate showing the respective tax authorities' evaluation of the building; the seller's declaration that they have paid all obligations to the state; and the seller's and buyer's declarations of their civil, family and property status.

The buyer is also responsible (unless otherwise agreed) for paying the notary tax for the deed (a sum fixed by government tables) and the land tax (2 per cent of the purchase price).

On the day of purchase, the notary registers the notary deed in the regional court's register of immovable properties. There will be a small tax payable for this. The buyer is responsible for negotiating and paying the notary's fees and those of his own lawyer and translator. Who pays the estate agent's fees is a matter of negotiation between buyer and seller.

If all this seems too daunting, Stara Planina Properties is a British-owned company set up to handle the purchase of property and its manaagment while the owners are away.

Romania

Ensure your estate agent is a member of UNAI (see page 125), which ensures that the property will have been properly vetted and you will be getting the best service. Although there is no obligation for a lawyer to be involved in the transaction, it is definitely worth employing one to be absolutely certain that you understand the procedure thoroughly and avoid any pitfalls.

The estate agent draws up the agreement between buyer and seller. If a deposit is paid, the amount is agreed between them. If the buyer reneges on the agreement, he forfeits the deposit. If the seller reneges, he must reimburse the buyer with a sum twice that of the deposit. It is the responsibility of the agent to undertake all the local searches, ensuring that all the requisite conditions are met.

The transfer of title and registration takes place in the presence of a notary. Every estate agent has a notary they work with, so once matters between buyer and seller are agreed, the notary gets the appropriate paperwork drawn up. All the parties concerned attend a meeting where the final contract is signed before the sale is registered with the Land Registry.

There are various hidden costs which will include the estate agent's fees, which can vary between 2 per cent (in Brasov) to 7 per cent (in Bucharest). The stamp and notary taxes are calculated on government tables which relate to the value of a property.

Useful Addresses

Bulgarian Embassy and Consulate General
186–188 Queen's Gate
London SW7 5HL
Tel: 020 7584 9400

Stara Planina Properties
Tel: 00 359 88 341694
www.stara-planina.com
A British-owned company that assists people looking to buy property in Bulgaria

Visa information service
01891 171208

Romanian Embassy and Consulate General
Arundel House, 4 Palace Green, London W8 4QD
Tel: 020 7937 9666 (embassy)
Tel: 020 7937 9667 (consulate general)

Romanian National Tourist Office
22 New Cavendish Street
London W1G 8TT
Tel: 020 7224 3692

Balkan Holidays
Sofia House, 19 Conduit Street
London W1S
Tel: 020 7543 5555
www.balkanholidays.co.uk

House-hunters

Right Linda and Tony were surprised to find a luxurious 1970s apartment inside this unprepossessing stone block.

Linda Lancaster and Tony Hayward

The last 'long and tedious' British winter was enough to drive Linda Lancaster and Tony Hayward abroad in search of a second home and some reliable weather. It was the first time they had visited Bulgaria but they were immediately charmed by its scenery, its sense of history and the low cost of living. More than that, it met their requirements of being 'mosquito-free and within reach of an airport easily accessible from the UK'. With a budget of £40,000, they started their search for a two- or three-bedroomed house, with a little garden that would maintain itself in their absence, which could double as a holiday home for their family.

The first property they saw was near Nesebâr, a popular base for upmarket holiday makers from Eastern Europe, known for its 19th-century wooden houses and windmills. The five-bedroomed villa had three bathrooms, a kitchen and a light living room with a balcony looking over the garden towards the forests and mountains. Outside, there was also a pool, a vineyard and a decrepid sauna. The décor was subdued but Linda and Tony thought the challenge of the garden would be invigorating. Unfortunately they were less keen on the surrounding area.

Next, they went inland to the sleepy town of Pet Mogili, named after the surrounding five hills which were neolithic burial mounds. Here a two-bedroomed farmhouse was on the market for a mere £6,500. In traditional Bulgarian style, it also had a large vineyard, an orchard and a vegetable garden, not forgetting the various outbuildings – and geese. The only thing it didn't have was a bathroom, and the outdoor toilet 'made those French holes in the floor look positively avant-garde'. Linda and Tony felt that it was a little primitive but they loved it. 'The rooms were roomy, it was very quaint and we fell in love with the garden.' They weren't so sure about the Bulgarian practice of using the toilet in the same place for 10 to 20 years before moving the whole thing to another spot though. However they were more reassured to hear that local builders would charge £1.50 per day for work to restore the place but, ultimately, they felt it would entail too much work so headed back to the coast, to the town of Varna.

Above A property in a Bulgarian village such as Pet Mogili, could provide a surprising opportunity for home buyers with a limited budget.

During the Communist regime, many blocks of flats here were built using concrete panels which has often resulted in severe structural problems. However there was a two-bedroomed apartment for sale at £29,000 in a stone block built by builders for themselves. The exterior was off-putting and the communal areas were dingy but once inside the flat, Linda and Tony were flabbergasted. It was an exercise in pure 1970s chic, with geometric wallpaper on the hall walls and ceiling, marble flooring throughout, underfloor heating and views across the rooftops. 'We loved it. It's so seedy on the outside, nobody in the world would guess what went on inside.' They were reliably informed that they should get £250 per month in rental although the agents would expect 50% of the first payment so longer lets were advisable. The only snag was that since the fall of Communism and the end of restrictions on living space, owners have been building out over their balconies. Apparently the government is cracking down on this development so it would be advisable for Linda and Tony to ensure the vendor got their extension legalised if they decided to buy the flat.

Their last port of call was an architect-designed, four-bedroomed house in Bliznatzi close to the beach at Kamichiya. Only seven years old, it had a split-level living/dining area and exclusive gardens which included a vineyard and orchard. Fully furnished, it was on the market for £31,000. 'We thought it was a lovely family house. We could live without a phone for a couple of years though we would want one eventually. But the location works against it.'

After some discussion Linda and Tony put in an offer on the flat in Varna but on return to the UK, were told that the asking price had suddenly been increased so they didn't proceed with the purchase. However their enthusiasm is undimmed and they are planning to return to the Black Sea Coast later in the year, determined to find a place in a country that they feel is brimming with opportunity.

> It was an exercise in pure 1970s chic, with geometric wallpaper on the hall walls and ceiling, marble flooring throughout and underfloor heating.

What can I take with me?

Moving house is always a testing time. It needs careful planning if it is to go without a hitch. Some holiday homes are sold fully furnished, in which case you will probably only need to worry about your pets, car and a few personal items. However, if you have an empty property waiting for your arrival, you have a more difficult task ahead.

It is worth checking with the relevant embassy or consulate whether there are any restrictions on bringing household goods from the UK into their country. Then decide how much you want to take. Be ruthless in sorting out your possessions. You do not want to saddle yourself with clothes or objects that would be better off in a charity shop or car-boot sale – and you certainly don't want to pay for their removal. It is worth getting three estimates from international removal companies. You need to know whether they will pack up your belongings for you, whether they will deal with any necessary paperwork connected with customs clearance, and whether they will transport your belongings all the way to your new home or leave them at the point of entry. If that is as far as they go, you will be expected to make the necessary arrangements to get everything through customs and organise onward transport from there.

To avoid any unnecessary problems it is advisable to choose a company that is an agent of the Federation of International Removers (FIDI) or Overseas Moving Network International (OMNI). They will be able to take you through your move step by step, look after the relevant paperwork (confirm that they do) and offer advice and shipping for pets and cars.

If you are not taking a great deal of possessions and are moving relatively close to the UK, you may prefer to economise by hiring a van and driving it to mainland Europe yourself. If you do, make sure to check the customs requirements of the countries that you pass through.

Make lists of what you want to take. Electrical appliances may not be compatible with your chosen country's voltage system, so you will have to replace yours when you get there. You may discover that it is cheaper to buy some things locally than going to the expense of shipping them over. Your removers may be able to advise you. Equally, there may be things you will need to buy here that are not available at your destination. Remember that you may need to have used them for six months in this country first if you are to avoid paying tax or duty. Find out what you can and cannot take into the country from the relevant Customs and Excise department.

All countries have rigorous import regulations when it comes to cars. You may find that the duty is too high to make it worthwhile taking one with you. Check with the relevant embassy to find out what restrictions exist. If you are moving to a country which drives on the right, a right-hand drive car is not ideal. It may be better to sell it and buy one when you arrive. However, if you cannot be parted from your trusty vehicle, find out where the nearest dealer service is to your new home. If the car breaks down or just needs servicing, it will be costly and time-consuming if you have to travel miles to get it fixed. Check whether your car will be more expensive to run in your destination country. Consider where you will be parking it – is your car too big for the available space?

If you plan to take your car abroad for more than 12 months, you have to apply for a certificate of export from the DVLA. If you do decide to trade in your car for another model before moving, the government runs a scheme whereby you can buy without VAT or car tax and use it in the UK for up to six months before it leaves the country. You can get details of the scheme from the Customs and Excise Office. Don't forget to check whether you need an international driving licence or whether your licence must be exchanged for a local one.

Before you make arrangements to take your pet abroad, contact the Ministry of Agriculture and ask if there are any restrictions on doing so. Some countries, for instance, will not admit certain breeds of dog. Legislation changes frequently and the Ministry will be completely up to date. If you are only going for weeks or months, your pet may need a pet passport. These are accepted by 25 countries and allow re-entry into the UK, although the animals are only accepted on certain routes. To get a passport, the animal needs to be micro-chipped, blood-tested, vaccinated against rabies and checked for ticks. Your vet must be an LVI (Local Veterinary Inspector) to do this. However, bear in mind that when the animal arrives at its destination, it may have to comply with the rules of that country regarding inoculations and other precautionary measures. If you are emigrating permanently, you will need an export health certificate and possibly other documentation, depending on the destination country. For these, contact your local Animal Health Divisional Office. If your removers do not carry animals, they may enlist another company who will have the proper facilities. Do check that they meet your expectations and that you feel comfortable about entrusting your pet to them. Moving is traumatic for your pet, so ask the vet's advice about whether it should be tranquillised to cope with the journey.

When moving your possessions, it is vital they are properly insured against loss, theft and breakage. Assuming they have been packed professionally, the shipment should withstand the worst knocks, but getting good cover will give you peace of mind. Make a complete inventory of everything you have packed so that you can check any discrepancies on arrival. This list is also useful for the removers to have when getting clearance through customs. If anything is damaged, it must be noted before you sign the delivery note. Check the small print of the agreement with the insurance company to make sure you understand their conditions.

Finally, don't forget to give the removers detailed instructions on how to find your house and make sure you are there when they arrive.

It is worth checking with the relevant embassy whether there are any restrictions on bringing household goods from the UK into their country. Then decide how much you want to take.

Florida

The sunshine state of Florida has been attracting tourists for years. In fact, it has been said that there is no such thing as a true Floridian since most of the people who live there were born outside the state. With year-round sunshine, a climate that varies from subtropical in the south to temperate in the north, Florida also offers a range of entertainment to suit everyone. Orlando is the theme park capital of the world, with Disney World, Universal Studios and Sea World providing the main attractions.

Along the coasts there are long, white-sanded beaches. In the north, quaint villages and deep forests are found in the Panhandle. The Florida Keys offer a Bohemian arts and crafts culture, while on the east coast there is the excitement of space-age Cape Canaveral. Go inland to central Florida for cattle ranches, lakeside communities and hours of fishing, golf or bird-watching. Travel south to the mangrove swamps of the Everglades for some alligator-spotting. Alternatively, try the buzz of cosmopolitan Miami, with its art deco hotels, renowned South Beach and its beautiful people. Who could ask for anything more?

Florida may be best known for Mickey Mouse and its rollercoaster rides but it has much more than that to offer to the thousands of Britons who flock to its sunshine every year. The standard of living is high and in property terms you can expect to get extremely good value for your money. Communications are excellent both within the state and with the rest of the world, and it is only an eight-and-a-half-hour flight away from the UK. Favourite destinations for British homebuyers are Orlando, southern Florida and the Gulf Coast, all of which have plenty to offer. However, the southern part of the state does get extremely hot and humid in the summer, with heavy rainfall in June and July. Homebuyers should also be aware of the risk of hurricanes, although the inhabitants of Florida are well-prepared with sophisticated tracking techniques, special insurance and building precautions.

Orlando is the number-one holiday destination and the place where businessman, Jeremy Mitchell, and his partner, Diane Maughan, came to find their dream home. 'We decided that we wanted to live in Florida because apart from the obvious, we love the relaxed, friendly atmosphere there. It's hard to describe, but when we have been there on holiday it felt like home.'

Once a quiet farming town, the city of Orlando has massively expanded over the last 20 years or so. Its downtown high-rise offices, and other buildings such as the Science Museum, contrast with elegant homes in residential areas set around lakes and parks. Despite a population of one million, the city has managed to retain a community feel, with plenty of boutiques, restaurants and cafés. Winter Park is one of the city's upmarket suburbs that has been a retreat for wealthy Floridians since the late-19th century. It is quiet, relaxed and home to the 100-year-old Rollins College. Its main street, Park Avenue, is lined with classy boutiques, smart restaurants and expensive gift shops.

Above *Apart from its 150 golf courses and family theme parks, Florida boasts 300 spring-fed inland lakes and waterways that provide a nature-lovers paradise where fishing, hiking and riding are among the many activities on offer.*

North of Orlando, in the heart of lush countryside, is the town of Mount Dora, small, amiable and full of southern charm. Its centre dates back to the 1800s when it was visited by President Thomas Jefferson. Up here, farming predominates over tourism and the easy-going pace of life in the neighbouring towns reflect that. Further north, Silver Springs and the Ocala National Forest are among Florida's popular natural attractions, providing opportunities for canoeing, cave-diving, swimming and hiking. The town of Ocala is in the heart of the horse-breeding district, where the hillsides are given over to hundreds of horse ranches and paddocks.

To the south of Orlando is theme-park land, where millions of people are entertained all year round. Kissimee, a resort town only 20 miles from Orlando, has doubled in size every decade since the arrival of the parks. Another town worth visiting is Celebration, which was created by Disney in 1996 to epitomise the American notion of community life. Designed to encourage neighbourliness, its traditional-style houses are built close to the roads, and, despite criticisms that it is soulless and contrived, it has a congenial atmosphere.

The rich farmland of central Florida is famous for its cattle ranches and orange groves. Among the many lakes and waterways is Lake Marian, just east of Lake Kissimee. Here, as elsewhere, affluent suburbs have grown up around the lake. This is the sort of area where your money will go further than if you were on the coast. It will buy you peace and quiet and sensational views across the water, with plenty of opportunities for bass fishing, boating and other watersports. Jenny Gerrard and her husband, Geoff, a bookie, looked at a secure, gated community here that offered a golf course, fitness centre, pool and children's play area – it seemed an idyllic place for a second home. 'I wanted to live in California but it was too expensive for us so we came to Florida. To my surprise, I have been so impressed. It's so clean – no graffiti or litter – and there's something about it that reminded us both of England 20 years ago in that sense of belonging and security. I felt safer walking down the road there than I sometimes do in Essex. We loved the simplicity of the Floridians who are unlike New Yorkers – more hick than slick, in the nicest possible way. We weren't particularly keen on the community resorts but we are going back to look at individual villas.'

Only an hour from Orlando is the famous Daytona Beach where Henry Ford and Louis Chevrolet, among others, put their prototype cars through their paces. As a legacy, the public are still allowed to drive on the beach – one of the few in Florida where this is permitted – and the world's fastest speedway is just a couple of miles away. This is where hordes of demob-happy students traditionally come for the spring break. The town council has tried to break with that custom, with the result that it's now a more modest resort but with rising property prices.

South of Daytona is the world-renowned Space Coast, so-called because it is home to the JF Kennedy Space Centre. The coastline around the Space Centre is totally unspoilt and is protected by the Merritt Wildlife Refuge and Canaveral National Seashore, which cover miles of swamp, savannah, marshland and beach. Just to the south is Cocoa Beach, the biggest beach in Florida and popular since the 1960s. These 10 miles of sand are not only the best place to see the space launches; they are also a surfer's paradise and provide excellent grounds for offshore fishing.

A rail link is being built from here to Orlando with a 15-minute shuttle to and from the theme parks. The port is also being expanded and in 10 years time will be the biggest cruise port in the world. Buying property here might well be a good investment. As the area opens up, so prices will rise. Inland there are several sleepy towns, largely populated by NASA's employees. Subsequently, they tend to have a strong community feel. Cocoa Village is the most attractive and has an old-fashioned, bohemian character with an easy-going atmosphere, and numerous arts and crafts shops.

Miami is one of the most stylish holiday destinations in America, despite its notoriously high crime rate. There's a wide cultural mix, a vibrant atmosphere and the temperature rarely drops below 80°F. This is where musician, Ric Halstead, and his wife, Nita, hoped to find a new home. 'After living abroad for 20 years, we find the UK is too expensive, too highly taxed for what you get and the weather is shocking. It's also been extremely difficult to start from scratch back here. I ran a club in Hong Kong

Above *Kissimee is a busy town where properties are well priced compared with the luxury developments that have grown up around it.*

Facts

State capital Tallahassee
Population 14,000,000
Land area 140,255 sq km
Currency 1 US dollar ($) = 100 cents
Electricity 110–115V
Time zone GMT – 5 hours
Religion Predominantly Protestant
Language English
Government Federal republic

Right Daytona Beach's reputation as a party town means that property here tends to be cheaper though prices have risen by about 20 per cent in the last few years.

Climate

Tampa

Average temperatures (°C)

Miami

Average temperatures (°C)

Orlando

Average temperatures (°C)

where I met many American musicians who made life in the States seem ideal. If we can get round the visa and work permit obstacles, I think it would suit us perfectly.'

Coral Gables is one of the historic districts where peaceful, tree-lined streets and Mediterranean-style architecture have attracted many wealthy residents. It was designed by George Merrick, who built Miracle Mile as a centrepiece, turned a huge quarry into the renowned Venetian Pool and revamped the construction ditches that circled the early town into a series of canals. Coral Gables has the status of a city within a city. It has its own mayor, town hall, police force and schools. If you buy here, you must observe the strict community rules which determine, for example, the colour of your house, the number of pets you own, and where you park your car.

Coconut Grove is another fashionable part of town and has been a popular resort since the late-19th century, when poets, writers and artists wintered here. Property is too expensive for struggling artists today, but many people are attracted by the buzz of the bohemian atmosphere. The streets are full of trendy boutiques, art galleries and outdoor cafés. The well-established Bahamian community has brought some of the flavour of the Bahamas with it.

The most glitzy place in Miami has to be Miami Beach. Connected to the mainland by a number of causeways, Miami Beach is a magnet for the 'beautiful people'. Yet only 100 years ago, much of the land was under water until Carl Fisher gave the financial backing to dredge Biscayne Bay and, with the help of circus elephants, used the landfill to landscape the island. In South Beach, pastel-coloured art deco hotels and apartment blocks line the sidewalks. It provides the hub of activity; with a reputation for being hedonistic, glamorous and gay, this is the place to party. To the north of the island are the exclusive enclaves of the wealthier members of the set, but it's possible to find sophisticated apartment complexes with every modern convenience laid on.

The west coast of Florida has as much to offer as the east. There's plenty of sun, empty white beaches and one of the lowest crime rates in America. Life here benefits not only from scuba diving, watersports and yachting, but also from the culture which is present in the museums, theatre and ballet companies, live music and new-age events. Tarpon Springs is a pretty Floridian town that was originally settled by fishermen from the Greek island of Kalymnos, who dived for sponges here. There's still a Greek feel to the town in its restaurants, its 19th-century brick streets and Greek

Orthodox church with its traditional Epiphany celebrations. New sponge beds were discovered in the 1980s, so the sponge docks are busy once again.

There are many new communities springing up along the coast. South of Tampa Bay lies Sarasota, the cultural capital of Florida. The Sarasota beaches have icing-sugar sands, while just out to sea are the upmarket Lido Key and Siesta Key, both accessible from the mainland by road. Siesta Key has a reputation for being expensive and exclusive, but affordable properties can still be found in this extremely desirable location. It's well worth exploring inland to find places virtually untouched by the tourist dollar.

The far south-west of the peninsula is one of Florida's best-kept secrets. It has remained largely undeveloped, though it has been attracting Americans on holiday for years. Greta Garbo and Gary Cooper used to come here in the golden days of Hollywood. This is where the 'snow birds' flock to – the senior citizens of the north who migrate with the birds to find winter sun where the temperature rarely drops below 70°F. It is a golfer's paradise, too. Fort Myers has a reputation as an up-and-coming good-time town enhanced by a number of apartment blocks, gift shops and beach bars.

South of the centre, it becomes quieter with protected beaches that are home to a variety of wildlife. Cape Coral is a new and relatively untapped area made in the 1950s by two developers who reclaimed 114 square miles of swamp for housing by digging out hundreds of miles of canals. The waterfront properties here are the cheapest you'll find in Florida and although the area boasts few amenities, it has the best boating facilities. The population has grown from zero to 100,000 in 40 years and there's certainly room for another 100,000. Down the coast, you come to the Gulf Coast's jewel in the crown, Naples. Its laid-back ambience is partly due to the age of its inhabitants who are largely retired – or thinking about retiring. The marina provides a haven for many yachtsmen, but the town is exclusive and less touristy than other areas on the coast, with real-estate prices rising by 95 per cent in the last decade.

Florida has so much to offer someone looking for a home in the sunshine, but it is vital to be aware of the ramifications of buying property there.

Above *Naples is a wealthy town, whose manicured beaches, exclusive shops and elegant restaurants ooze money and class.*

How to get there

Air
American Airlines fly direct from Heathrow to Miami. British Airways fly Heathrow to Miami; Gatwick to Tampa and Orlando. Virgin Atlantic fly Gatwick to Orlando twice daily; Gatwick to Miami; Manchester to Orlando (May to November only). Charter flights operate from various UK airports to Orlando, Miami, Tampa, Naples, Sarasota among others. Flight time: 9 hours

How to buy property in...
Florida

Buying property in Florida is highly regulated and quite different from buying property in the UK, so it is important you seek good independent advice to ensure you avoid any pitfalls. Try to find a suitable lawyer or realtor recommended by other expatriates and certainly shop around until your are satisfied with their terms and reputation.

There is a central register of all properties for sale known as the MLS (Multiple Listing Service), to which member realtors have access. Use one realtor in the area you like; with several kinds available you need to be certain which responsibilities yours will shoulder. Do not sign anything that commits you to your realtor as this is unnecessary. A buyer's broker has a duty to look after buyers even though the seller is responsible for payment of the sale fee.

You can view any number of properties for sale regardless of where the property instructions originate; if a purchase results with additional realtor involvement, a split commission is arranged between them. Ask your prospective realtor if they hold a Florida Real Estate Commission licence (FREC). If they do, this will protect your interests because they are obliged to act under a code of conduct and you can be reimbursed if you suffer losses because of unprofessional behaviour.

If, as a result of the restricted immigration laws (see pages 68–69), you decide like most non-residents to rent out the property you buy, it is vital to check the existing and planned regulations on short-term lets. Many regions in Florida are zoned and short-term letting restrictions are common in many cities,

communities or counties. In some places you may not be able to rent out your property at all. Even if there is no zoning at present, you will still need to consider the implications if this were ever to change at a future date.

The reason for these restrictions is that many full-time residents object and hotels want a monopoly on short-term accommodation. Remember, not every location in Florida will enable mortgage repayments to be covered by rental income. If you wish to let your property, besides choosing a suitable property and location, take great care in your choice of management company. It is unwise to rely on any future rental income to pay for a purchase as there can never be a foolproof guarantee.

It is always essential to obtain independent advice, especially when the sales company provides their own management service as the two operations often conflict. It is vitally important to check for inflated rental projections and question any so-called 'guarantees'. If you rent out a property for more than 14 days, you must file a US tax return and pay tax on the income, although there is a US–UK tax treaty preventing double taxation and you can offset mortgage costs and travel expenses. It is essential to obtain specialist accountancy advice. As rental income is normally paid in dollars, a fluctuating exchange rate should only impact on your deposit should you be fortunate enough to generate sufficient rental income to cover the purchase costs.

It is also important to ascertain if there are any community restrictions on a property. This may forbid you to hang washing outside, prescribe the colour of the exterior, and so on. Will living within these confines suit your lifestyle?

Having selected a realtor or broker in your area, expect them to be far more involved in the process than a UK estate agent. They will show a buyer around various properties; then, once a property is chosen, they will submit the offer to the vendor's agent. If it is accepted, possibly after some negotiation on which they may advise, they will draw up a contract between the buyer and vendor subject to any conditions specified by the buyer. These can include being subject to survey, finance agreements or a termite check (common on old properties in Florida). Some conditions may be required by law; others will be suggested by your agent or lender. The contract will also state how the closing costs will be paid since they are a matter of negotiation. It should also state exactly what is being sold, and whether any furniture, outbuildings and land are included. When the buyer is satisfied that the contract contains all the necessary conditions and clauses to protect him – ideally in consultation with an independent legal adviser – then he must sign and leave a deposit.

While shopping around for the best mortgage deal or arranging your finances, buyers should be aware that owner's title insurance will be required to ensure against any future claim by a third party. It is also worthwhile taking legal advice at this stage on gift and inheritance tax and their implications. If buying a new property, ensure the building costs are paid and that the contract relating to your property and purchase has been approved by a lawyer qualified in US contracts.

When the offer is accepted and finance obtained, the process is handed over to the closing agents or title company; these are independently operated and are similar to an insurance company. They ensure there is clear title to the property and check for any debts, restrictions or easements such as rights of way. Just before completion, return to the property to check everything is as it should be according to the contract. Now is the moment to ask the vendor to put anything right. The completion of the contract will be carried out in a meeting between the title company, the buyer and seller, the realtors, any lawyers, and representatives of the mortgage company or bank. On signing the contract, the money will be transferred to the vendor and the keys handed over to the buyer.

You should expect hidden charges to amount to approximately 5 per cent of the purchase price. These may include legal fees, the title search, title insurance surveyor's costs, home owners' insurance and mortgage tax, although in the case of a new home the builder often contributes to these costs. Be prepared to pay property tax annually; the amount varies between 1 and 3 per cent depending on the location of the property, and is used to finance local services.

It is impossible to deal here with every issue that may arise. What is important is that you do your homework, seek advice from independent realtors, other expatriates, your solicitor, the immigration authorities and an experienced US financial/ mortgage advisor before you make a purchase. But if you are scrupulously thorough and are clear about what you want, you will soon find yourself on the yellow brick road to your American dream.

House-hunters

Sue and Dave Lewinton

Two years ago Sue and Dave Lewinton decided to retire to the Sunshine Coast for six months every year. Before doing anything else, they opened a US bank account and obtained a US driving licence. They then spent a month looking at locations, starting at Naples and driving north, staying a couple of nights at the places they liked on the way. 'We fell in love with Sarasota and Tarpon Springs and saw between 25 and 30 properties, but none of them felt quite right.'

They knew exactly what they wanted – a minimum of three bedrooms, a caged pool and a double garage. They saw four very different houses that fell within their £120,000 budget. The first was a four-bedroomed luxury villa in Tarpon Springs which backed on to a nature reserve and was five minutes from the beach. It was reasonably priced at £113,000, with two bathrooms, two reception rooms, a double garage, a covered porch, a garden and a caged, solar-heated pool. 'It's a lovely location and has everything we need and more – the heated pool, the extra bedroom, the high cathedral ceilings. It's perfect for us.'

Next they saw a two-bedroomed Sears kit house in Sarasota which had been built in 1925. It had kept its original mouldings and heart pine floor, had a one-bedroomed guesthouse in the garden and was on the market for £113,000. But, despite its character, it was not for Dave and Sue. 'It's extremely unusual and not what we expected. It could make a lovely home but we definitely want a pool and a garage.'

For something quite different, they looked at a waterfront condominium in the Bay Oaks development in Siesta Key. At £132,500, it was over their budget but the place is a sailor's paradise, with a private dock outside the back door. This was a one-bedroomed, ground-floor apartment with a large open-plan living area, a bright, well-equipped kitchen, sea views and access to the communal pool and gardens. 'It's a fabulous location but without as much space as we'd have liked. The rental opportunities may be great but we're not planning on renting so it's not a consideration.'

FInally, they looked at a three-bedroomed house in Palm Harbour. It had everything the couple wanted, with immaculate detailing throughout and four reception rooms including a formal dining room at the reasonable price of £113,000. 'It's in good condition, perfect, but it's very dark inside and only 150 yards from Route 19. The traffic noise would be overwhelming.'

After filming *A Place in the Sun*, Dave and Sue stayed on another week, viewing

Below After painstaking research and viewing a number of properties, Sue and Dave settled on this luxury villa.

Above *The large, covered poolside area is ideal for entertaining friends and family.*

another 15 or so houses. On the following Tuesday morning they made up their minds to offer on the first house they'd seen on the programme. Their realtor, Joan Dvorak (from the Clearwater office of RE/MAX) gave them a list of prices that other properties in the area had sold for as a guide.

'On Wednesday morning we met Joan and she drew up the contract of everything we were prepared to offer and faxed it to the buyer's realtor saying we had to hear back by 5pm that day because we were leaving on Friday. At 4pm we heard they had accepted our offer. Joan immediately booked a surveyor, who we met the next morning at the house. He went over it thoroughly with us and typed his report up overnight so it was at Joan's office on Friday morning. We paid a deposit of $1,000 and flew home to arrange a further deposit of $10,000 within the next 10 days. Because we had a US name account we could then transfer the balance of the money when the dollar was right for us.'

Two months later they flew back and did a 'walk through' to check the property was in the condition they expected. In fact, the mechanics of the pool needed attention, so while they were at the meeting at the title company, the vendor left an open cheque with his realtor to put it right. 'We paid with a banker's draft and the house was ours in half an hour!' During the three days previously, the Lewintons signed up with all the utility companies (water, electricity and garbage), had the carpets cleaned and bought a bed which was delivered one day later – the first day in their new home.

'It's a lovely location and has everything we need and more – the heated pool, the extra bedroom, the high cathedral ceilings. It's perfect for us.'

Florida . . . .

House-hunters

Bill and Carol Giles

Carol and her husband, Bill, know Florida well. 'We've visited several times and promised ourselves that when we retired we would have an eternal summer, spending six months in Florida and six in England. Last year was very traumatic healthwise and we made up our minds to go for something today rather than tomorrow.'

'We're close to Tampa for theatres and Clearwater Beach is one of the nicest beaches in Florida. We've pursued our dream of thirty years and at long last it's coming true.'

Carol went hunting with her daughter, Helen, quite clear that she wanted to find a three-bedroomed, two-bathroomed villa with a private pool within their budget of £100,000. They first saw a two-bedroomed show flat in the Naples' Vanderbilt Country Club. On the market for £100,000, it had two bathrooms, a fitted kitchen, open-plan living area and a screened balcony overlooking the golf course. It had access to the Club's heated pools, fitness centre, tennis courts, golf course and clubhouse. The apartment itself was well designed, light and attractive, and displayed all the upgrades (such as splashbacks and mirror panelling) which would cost another £9,000; the furniture package would cost an additional £28,000. In a short-term rental zone, it had high rental potential. But it lacked the extra bedroom and private pool on which Carol had her heart set.

On to Fort Myers, where they saw another two-bedroomed apartment in the Sands Condominium Complex with access to the heated pool – and the daily aerobic workout – and only a short walk from the beach. It was on the market for £86,500. There were a number of deed restrictions on the property

which, among other things, limited the size of pets, forbade cardigans on chairs, cigarettes on the lawn, glasses by the pool, hanging washing outside and having more than six people to stay. These draconian regulations didn't entirely put Carol off. 'It's very spacious inside with big bedrooms and beautiful views. It's very rentable but a bit too small. Besides, I don't want to have to get my hair done every day after the water aerobics!'

The next possibility came as a rather a shock. It was a two-bedroomed trailer home on Goodman Island – waterfront living at its most relaxed and a steal at £100,000. It came with a screened patio, its own dock, two storage sheds, a carport and was fully furnished. Perhaps the best thing about it was the views across the sea towards the Gulf of Mexico. There were no

rental or deed restrictions, but it was in a hurricane zone. Carol was horrified by the thought of regular evacuations. 'Otherwise it's very quaint and reminds me of old Florida. If we were only interested in mooring a boat it would be ideal. My husband would love it, but you would have to pay me to live there.'

Finally, she looked at a four-bedroomed family home overlooking a canal in Cape Coral. For £97,500 it had a large, fully-equipped kitchen, an airy living room, two bathrooms, a huge screened patio, a private pool and direct access to the canal. Carol's verdict? 'Fantastic. This is the dream home we've been looking for.' However, before they made an offer, Carol and Helen went to Clearwater, where they found perfection. An English estate agent, FI Grey, had tipped her off about a new gated community. They saw a show house and inspected the many amenities – golf course, tennis courts, restaurant and more. But rather than taking them in, all Carol could think about was she and Bill sharing their first glass of champagne in the spa. Although well over their original budget, she has bought a house off-plan in a stunning conservation area with protected views. Carol and Helen tied everything up within one week, using both an American and English lawyer to advise them. Payments will be made in agreed stages and Carol hopes their new home will be ready in nine months, complete with pool and spa.

'A new road is being built from Tampa airport so it will only be a 20-minute drive. This is far enough away from Disney World but near enough for when our grandchildren visit. We're close to Tampa for theatres, to Newport Richie for open-air concerts. The shopping malls and discount warehouses are nearby and Clearwater Beach is one of the nicest beaches in Florida. We've pursued our dream of 30 years and at long last it's coming true.'

Above *When Carol looked round this show house in a new development, she knew she'd found the place of her dreams.*

Opposite *Carol and her daughter Helen during filming.*

Making yourself at home

At last you have arrived at your dream home. All the hurdles of finding it, funding it, purchasing it, restoring it and leaving home are over. But there are one or two things that are still left to do, though you will probably have prepared for them.

Make sure you have notified the mains companies of the date of your arrival so the water, gas, electricity and telephone are connected. Now is the time to open a bank account, if you haven't already. If moving permanently, you may want to register with a local doctor and dentist, giving them your records if necessary.

If you are moving abroad with young children, this may be the time to enrol them in the local primary school. Generally speaking, children pick up a new language quickly and will be chattering fluently in both languages before the term is out. If your children are older, you will need to investigate the secondary-school situation as a priority. If they are fluent in the language, they may also fit in to a local school. Alternatively, you may prefer to send them to an international school. Such schools are generally found in major towns or in areas where there are large expatriate communities.

The one other family member that may need time to adjust to this new way of life is your pet. You should check whether or not it needs particular vaccinations or tagging once it has arrived. Otherwise you may find that it needs

time to settle after the trauma of the journey. Make sure it can't escape from your house and garden for the first couple of weeks so that it familiarises itself with its new home and can easily find its way back.

To make yourself really at home, it is essential to learn the language of the country you are moving to. You may have begun before you left by taking evening classes, enrolling in a crammer course at a local language school or teaching yourself through the many courses available on audio tape, video and CD that are supplemented by various books and exercises. It will help if you can practise with a friend or partner. Once you have a working knowledge of the language, you can boost it by watching foreign-language cable TV programmes or by tuning into local radio stations.

However, there is nothing like living in a country for learning a language colloquially and quickly. The key is not to be afraid to try. Nobody is going to laugh at you for having a go. In fact, quite the reverse. Most people will appreciate the efforts you make to speak their language and will help you as much as they can. It's certainly the first step to making some new friends among the local community. Begin gradually, breaking yourself in with shopping and moving on to more complicated exchanges, perhaps with your neighbours.

Having uprooted yourself from your friends and family at home, you are bound to miss

What is the point of moving to a different country if you don't experience the people and the culture? If you make an effort to join the local community, you will almost certainly be welcomed in.

them. Of course, they will visit you when they can but you will almost certainly want to build up a new network of friends and acquaintances, integrating yourself into the local community.

If you have chosen a resort complex or sheltered accommodation, you are likely to meet other British people who will share your enjoyment of the facilities on offer. Children are often key to making family friends. After a couple of days in the pool they will be familiar with lots of other children and gradually you will meet their parents. Another way to bring you into contact with others is to join classes or activities, whether water aerobics, skiing or golf (there are likely to be plenty of opportunities on offer, unless you have opted for a remote hideaway). The other must is not to wait until your neighbours make contact with you. Don't be shy – invite them round for a house-warming drink. It could mark the start of a long friendship.

The disadvantage of living in a resort community is that it can be difficult to meet local people or absorb the authentic flavour of the country. If you limit yourself to the local expatriates, you may find yourself in a small pool of people with whom you have little in common apart from your native country. And, some would ask, what is the point of moving to a different country if you don't experience the people and the culture? If you make an effort to join the local community, you will almost certainly be welcomed in. It may be that you shop locally, take your children to the local school, or that you are trying to establish a business; gradually you will become integrated into the community, especially if you speak the language.

Don't transfer a British 'couch potato' way of life overseas. Take advantage of the new opportunities offered to you by meeting new people, exploring the country, sharing the local food and wine, and enjoying the culture. It is important to try to put something back into the community that you have joined, perhaps through employing local labour (builder, gardener or cleaner), using local facilities or supporting local schemes. If you have children in the local primary school, you will soon meet other parents and be invited to join in with the school activities.

If you live among the local community, you may find it harder to find English-speaking friends. However, they should be easy enough to contact. In a small place they will probably make themselves known to you, whereas in a larger town or on an island, there are often clubs or organisations for British people living abroad (your estate agent is bound to know if that's the case), and local expatriate news sheets. If you make an effort, it won't be long before you will have established a different lifestyle with new friends and you will be in a position to get the most from your very own place in the sun.

Making yourself at home

Eastern Caribbean

ention 'Caribbean islands' and people immediately conjure up visions of palm-fringed, white, sandy beaches; clear aquamarine waters and dense rainforest; the taste of rum punch, the sound of steel drums, the reggae beat and a relaxed and tranquil way of life. The islands in the Eastern Caribbean offer all these pleasures and more. Each one has its own distinct character: some such as Anguilla, Antigua or Barbados are low-lying, while many of the others such as St Lucia or Monserrat are volcanic in origin and boast mountainous, rain-forested interiors.

Culturally, the islands owe their differences to their former colonial allegiances. French language, customs and food are evident in the French Antilles; Dutch prevails in the Netherlands Antilles; and British-style politics, Anglican churches and the familiar sound of leather on willow are found on the islands with a British heritage. Everywhere brilliant-coloured houses in pinks, blues, reds and greens stand out under trees groaning with avocados, coconuts, papaya, mangoes and spices. Among the islands there are some of the best snorkelling and dive sites in the world, with wonderful opportunities for sailing and watersports. If you want to take life easy, this could be the place for you.

*A*fter years of occupation and foreign rule, the Eastern Caribbean now has eight independent states, plus the French départements of Guadaloupe (including St Barts and north St Martin) and Martinique; the UK dependencies of Monserrat and Anguilla; and the Dutch dependencies of Saba, St Eustatius and South St Martin.

With this cultural diversity and geographical variation, the islands have maintained their differences: St Kitts and Nevis are renowned for their old world charm; Antigua is rich in colonial history with a beach for every day of the year; and Dominica is known as the 'Nature Island' because its spectacular scenery provides activities for hikers, divers and naturalists. Guadaloupe's lively blend of French, African and Indian cultures expresses itself in the Creole language and cuisine; Martinique, once known as 'Island of Flowers', is decidedly French in influence; and Monserrat is referred to as the 'Emerald Isle', not only both because of its fertile interior but also because of the influence of the early Irish migrants. Saba, the tip of an underwater mountain, is known as the 'Unspoiled Queen', and Barts has an untainted, Mediterranean feel. The list goes on and on. *A Place in the Sun* visited four islands looking for individual dream homes.

St Lucia

St Lucia is one of the most relaxed and friendly of the Caribbean islands, with year-round sun, 40 miles of sandy beaches and a welcoming atmosphere. There are constant reminders that it is a volcanic island – the sulphurous smell of the inland bubbling volcano crater and the twin peaks of the Pitons that rear 600 metres out of the sea by the sleepy south-western coast town of Soufrière.

Below Marigot Bay has an idyllic natural harbour with a marina overlooked by villas dotted on the hills above.

The island has had a troubled history, particularly while the British and the French fought for its possession. Between 1746 and 1814, the island changed hands 14 times until the British finally took control. The legacy of this struggle is a vibrant Creole culture – an intriguing blend of French, British and African traditions.

The laid-back capital town of Castries is built around a natural deep-water harbour, which has been a busy port for centuries. Now it is a stop-over for Caribbean cruise ships and the container ships that transport bananas, tropical fruits and spices. The town has lost some of its classic Caribbean character as a result of four major fires, the last in 1948. But it is still possible to enjoy local West Indian culture, particularly at the busy fruit and vegetable market, and in Columbus Square where a few wooden buildings and the cathedral have survived. High on the hill behind the town stands Fort Charlotte, which was built by both the French and English because of its strategic position. Today it is used as a school.

The coast north of Castries is the most popular with holidaymakers. The centre of their activities is the marina town of Rodney Bay, named after the British general who finally defeated the French. The land was only recovered from swampland in 1970 but is now a busy centre for many water-based activities, with nearby Pigeon Island providing the setting for the annual Jazz Festival.

The long beach, calm waters and relaxed atmosphere attract many people, with the result that property is expensive in this area. Just inland is the shanty fishing town of Gros Islet, which bursts into life every Friday night with street music and dancing in the 'jump-up'.

The new road south from Castries passes banana plantations and fishing villages until it reaches Marigot Bay. Continuing south is Soufrière, the first town built on the island by the French in 1746. It still has many of its wooden buildings intact and is only a water taxi ride away from Anse Chastenet, where some of the best diving in St Lucia can be had. Further inland are the island's botanical gardens with mineral baths, sulphur springs and various working plantations. Savannes Bay lies on the south-east coast, close to the international airport that was built by the Allies during the Second World War. There are fishing villages and sandy beaches in this unspoilt area, which is being designated as St Lucia's first national park. It is currently being developed and the Castles in Paradise complex is the first of its kind on this part of the island.

For something completely different, away from the calm Caribbean waters and the crash of the Atlantic ocean, it's possible to find much cheaper property inland, though the rental opportunities are limited. Babonneau, in the north of the island, is where the Empress Josephine, wife of Napoleon, was born in 1763. It's one of the poorest places on the island but Babonneau – or other similar villages – would guarantee an authentic Caribbean experience, where locals speak in patois and lead a traditional, relaxed way of life.

The native cuisine of St Lucia features lots of fresh fish, including blue fish, king fish, tuna and conch, callalloo soup (similar to spinach), curries, pepperpot stews and a wide variety of tropical fruit. Piton, the local beer, is brewed in Vieux Fort and if you are looking for something stronger, try one of the St Lucian rums.

Facts: Grenada

Capital St George's
Population 89,000
Land area 340 sq km
Currency 1 East Caribbean
   dollar (EC$) = 100 cents
Electricity 110v
Time zone GMT – 5 hours
Religion About half Roman
   Catholic
Language English
Government Constitutional
   monarchy with
   Westminster-style
   parliament

Below After two devastating fires in the 18th century, wooden houses were banned in St George's so most homes are built in brick or stone, with orange tiled roofs.

Grenada

Known as the 'spice island' because of its spice production, Grenada is one of the most unspoilt islands in the Eastern Caribbean. In the 16th century, homesick Spanish sailors named it Grenada after the southern Spanish town. When the French took control, they changed the name to Grenade, but the British had the last say, altering it to Grenada (pronounced Gren-ay-da).

The island's volcanic origins are evident: the capital town of St George's is clustered around one extinct crater, which forms the deep natural harbour, while inland the highest point of Mount St Catherine is another. The island is divided into six parishes, beginning with St Patrick in the north through St Mark, St Andrew, St John, and St George to St David in the south. The southern coast is punctuated with headlands and bays, which makes it particularly popular with sailors; inland, dense rainforest is cut with glittering rivers and waterfalls. Cloves, cinnamon, mace, nutmeg and ginger scent the air.

Environmentalist, Adrian Wilkes, came to the island from London in search of a different climate and lifestyle. He was looking to continue much of

Climate

Castries

Average temperatures (°C)

St George's

Average temperatures (°C)

Bridgetown

Average temperatures (°C)

his work via the internet and become involved in some of the educational and rehabilitation work being carried out in the environmental station on the island. 'Grenada has all the benefits of the Caribbean climate, with year-round sunshine, warm water, beautiful beaches, stunning countryside, friendly people and a relaxed lifestyle. The other important reason I chose it is because it is still relatively undeveloped, without any of the mass tourism that some other islands suffer from.'

St George's is one of the most picturesque towns in the Caribbean. The waterfront of Carenage is regularly visited by cruise ships, while the pastel-coloured Georgian townhouses rise up the hill behind it in a warren of narrow streets. For a taste of colourful Grenadian life, there's the busy fruit and spice market in the market square. To the south of the town is a huge expanse of sandy beach at Grand Anse backed by hills dotted with buildings. This end of the island, which includes the secluded Morne Rouge Bay and the more wealthy Lance aux Épines, is most popular with visitors and this is reflected in the property prices.

The parish of St David's in the south-east doesn't have a main town – just a scattering of houses – but it does exult in a stunning coastline fringed by an abundance of tropical fruit and spice trees. This is one of the hottest places to buy property at the moment. However, if you are looking for traditional colonial houses, they are hard to come by on Grenada because they are not protected; many are derelict because of neglect or because of prohibitively high restoration costs. In the northern-most parish of St Patrick's – the oldest rum producing district of the Caribbean – is the town of Sauteurs. It gets its name from the French verb *sauter* (to jump), because in 1651, rather than submit to the French, the last Carib natives leapt from the cliffs to the their death. Until recently the town could only be reached by boat. Like the rest of the island, the area is protected from development by strict planning restrictions. While property is cheap here, the market is slow and rental possibilities are more limited.

Off the north-east coast, a short boat-ride away, lies the tiny uncrowded island of Carriacou, where life exists much as it did 100 years ago. A magnet for divers and yachtsmen, it offers possibilities for a perfect island hideaway.

Grenada is only a 10-hour flight from the UK. It offers watersports, game fishing and good hiking along the trails of the Grand Étang National Park. It even has a nine-hole golf course. But most of all it offers tranquillity, matchless scenery and a completely different way of life.

Barbados

One hundred miles east of the Windward Islands, Barbados was claimed in 1625 by the British, who ruled until the island became an independent nation in 1966. The British have left a legacy of cricket, Anglican churches, place names and even polo. These days Barbados is one of the most popular islands in the Caribbean for British holidaymakers and house-hunters alike. Perhaps this is not surprising as the weather is consistently warm (July is the wettest month). Its white sands and rolling rural interior make it a dream location for a second home.

Barbados is divided into eleven parishes, from St Lucy in the north to Christchurch in the south. Bridgetown is the island's busy, modern capital that is built up around the Careenage, an inlet near the inviting sands of Carlisle Bay. In the 17th century, the booming sugar and slave trades brought prosperity to the town, but most of the merchants' splendid homes and warehouses were destroyed in a fire in 1860. Now the city is made up of attractive colonial-style buildings with more modern blocks mixed in. North of the town are a couple of rum factories, one of which is the internationally renowned Mount Gay. Further south, past Garrison Savannah, is the town of Hastings, once the British military headquarters and now a venue for cricket and horse racing.

A Place in the Sun

In the 1970s, this was one of the first places on the island to be developed as a tourist resort, although its original appeal is now sadly lacking.

The tranquil resort of Silver Sands on the southern tip is Barbadian in flavour, though British visitors leave the main tourist trail to come here. There's a fishing harbour with a market and plenty of inexpensive fish restaurants. Popular with the surfing community, this is an up-and-coming area where new developments are being built. North of Bridgetown, the west coast boasts stunning white beaches, which have been a magnet to the rich and famous. Consequently, this seven-mile stretch is known as the Platinum Coast and boasts many luxurious hotels – notably the Sandy Lane – and designer shopping. Mostly in the parish of St James, the land near the coast is extremely expensive, although cheaper, more modest options do come up.

Inland, the scenery is curiously reminiscent of the agricultural landscape of Kent and Surrey, but with the smell of sugar cane lingering in the air. It is surprising that more British don't look for property here in such an apparently familiar location.

Fish, particularly flying fish, is a main staple of the Bajan cuisine, though chicken and steak feature strongly. The national dish is *cou-cou*, an okra and cornmeal pudding, and there is a riot of wonderful tropical fruit to choose from. Banks is the local beer but Barbados is much more famous for its rum, which you can buy from tiny rum shops dotted throughout the island. With the strains of Calypso ringing in your ears, where better to search out your own place in the sun?

Tobago

Tobago is the smaller part of Trinidad and Tobago, the two-island nation at the southern end of the Caribbean island chain that was once part of the land mass of Venezuela. Tobago offers the quiet attractions of glorious beaches, coral reefs and the oldest protected rainforest in the western hemisphere. Trinidad, in contrast, is loud, exuberant, multicultural and host to the world-famous Carnival that centres on its capital, Port of Spain. Their history is as different as their characters. Although both

Above The east side of Barbados attracts less development because of its craggy coast and the pounding Atlantic waves.

Facts: Trinidad & Tobago

Capital Port of Spain
Population 1,176,000
Land area 5,128 sq km
Currency 1 Trinidad and Tobago dollar (TT$) = 100 cents
Electricity 110v
Time zone GMT – 5 hours
Religion Non-denominational
Language English
Government Parliamentary democracy

Air
British Airways and BWIA West Indies Airlines operate flights from London to St Lucia, Barbados, Grenada and Trinidad. Charter flights are available from other airlines. LIAT is the Caribbean's main inter-island carrier, connecting 25 destinations.
Flight time: 8 ½–9 ½ hours.

Boat
The Eastern Caribbean boat service also operates daily between the islands.

Below *Pigeon Point: pour a glass of rum, dip your toes in the water and enjoy the sunset.*

were claimed by the Spanish when Columbus sighted them, no attempts were made to colonise Tobago, with the result that the English, French, Dutch and Latvians decided to battle it out for control. By 1814, when it was finally ceded to the British, Tobago had changed hands no less than 31 times.

The island has a high mountainous spine, which is interrupted by river valleys running down to a coast that is dimpled with bays and coves. Most tourist activity centres on the low-lying western tip of the island near the popular beaches of Store Bay and palm-fringed Pigeon Point. Inland, you'll find traditional, rural Tobago dotted with banana homesteads, lush farms and small villages where property prices are cheaper than on the coast.

The lowlands extend north until they reach Plymouth on the west coast and the lively island capital of Scarborough on the east. Scarborough's clapboard houses surround the harbour and hectic market place, climbing the hill past a few colonial buildings to Fort St George, with its panoramic view across the island and out to sea. The windward coast has plenty of attractive beaches, but the choppy Atlantic can make them less safe for swimming. The best dive sites on the island are off the two north coast villages of Speyside, with its painted buildings surrounding a large playing field, and Charlotteville, an active fishing village situated round Man of War Bay.

The main attractions of the island include snorkelling in the Buccoo Reef National Park, hiking through the highland Tobago Forest Reserve and visits to the Argyle Falls and the Kings Bay Falls. When you have worked up an appetite, sample some of the local dishes such as crab and dumpling, macaroni pie with callaloo and curried goat. When it comes to Tobago, there's no doubt that small *is* perfect.

How to buy property in the...
Eastern Caribbean

Before buying property in the Caribbean, you should instruct a solicitor in the UK or the Caribbean to handle the process and advise against any pitfalls. On most islands the purchase process follows the British system, where negotiations are conducted between the buyer and seller through the agent, and terms are agreed subject to an exchange of contract. After this, further investigations are conducted before a completion of the contract takes place. Pre-contract enquiries include local searches, and post-contract investigations will look into the title of the property and the vendor's capacity to sell. However, there are various additional requirements and variations that must be observed depending on the individual islands.

St Lucia

People from overseas require an Alien's Landholding Licence to purchase property on the island. The licence is granted for a specific property only. You will need a local lawyer to deal with licence applications, carry out the searches and draw up the deed of sale. The lawyer might be recommended by your estate agent, a fellow expatriate, or a solicitor in the UK. A licence fee of 10 per cent is payable plus a £50 application fee, legal fees and stamp duty (2 per cent of the purchase price). The land or house is secured by the payment of a 25 per cent non-returnable deposit 60 days after signature of a contract of sale, by which time all searches and surveys need to be completed. If you buy land, it must be developed within two years of purchase. Thereafter, there are no restrictions on renting or selling.

Barbados

There are no restrictions on foreign nationals buying in Barbados, but the purchase must be registered with the Exchange Authority Commission. Expect legal fees to be about 1.5 per cent of the purchase price and a land tax to be levied which varies on the value of the property and the time of transaction.

Grenada

Foreigners wishing to purchase property in Grenada are allowed to own property upon payment of an aliens' landholding tax (currently 10 per cent of the selling price). Formalities are minimal but can take up to three months to process. Your lawyer will handle the paperwork, which must include police clearance from the UK, a banker's reference and a character reference. The price of the application is EC$1,800. Other hidden costs include legal fees, stamp duty (1 per cent of purchase price), government fees of EC$250 and payment of 5 per cent of your legal fees to the government. You must have a survey to apply for the Alien Landholder's Licence, but be warned – it will not come cheap.

Trinidad and Tobago

Foreigners are allowed to purchase up to one acre for residential purposes and up to five acres for commercial purposes. If the property exceeds this, permission will have to be received from the Ministry of National Security. Purchasing a house or land does not automatically confer resident status – this depends on the number of years spent in the country. A non-resident should be able to get a visa for three months. Extensions can be applied for, though they are not necessarily granted. Seek advice from the Trinidad and Tobago High Commission if you are concerned about immigration or work permit requirements. The buyer pays 10 per cent on signature of the sales agreement. Once good title is established, usually within 90 days, the balance is paid. Legal fees and stamp duty (7–10 per cent between them) and fire insurance (if buying a house) are due at this stage.

House-hunters

'The people here are so friendly and, of course the rum's cheap. But more than anything, it's the people – they make you feel so welcome.'

Below Peter and Sally enjoying a Caribbean holiday.

Peter Sullivan and Sally Turner

Seventeen years ago, self-employed heating and plumbing engineer, Peter Sullivan, first visited Barbados and fell in love with it. 'The people here are so friendly and, of course the rum's cheap. But more than anything, it's the people – they make you feel so welcome.' He introduced his partner, lecturer Sally Turner, to the island in 1997, taking her to all his favourite places and introducing her to the many friends he'd made there. 'Despite the long friendships that have developed, we still manage to disagree over who is the better cricket team. Thankfully, these debates usually take place over a few beers at Buffy's rum shop.' Sally was immediately smitten, too. After many holidays here, they decided to buy an island hideaway which they would use for one month and then rent out for the rest of the year. 'Ideally we're looking for a two-bedroomed property with a bit of garden if we can afford it. It should give us a bit of extra income, but it's also an investment for our future so one day we'll be able to buy something bigger and more permanent.'

The island has a reputation for being expensive but, as Peter and Sally, armed with a £90,000 budget, were to find out, this is not necessarily the case. The first port of call was on the celebrated coastline of St James. In a quiet suburb they found a three-bedroomed house with two terraces, a garage and a garden with room for a pool. The rooms were spacious and cooled by a gentle breeze. Like most of the houses in Barbados it ran on solar power. In good structural order, it only needed some cosmetic work, including a change of decoration to the very pink bathroom. On the market

for £100,000, including the furniture, it seemed well priced in such a prestigious area. Prices are constantly on the up here so this would almost certainly represent a good investment and have good rental potential. Sally liked the fact that it was so spacious and was only a short walk from the beach, but she was put off by it being in such a residential area.

So it was on to Silver Sands, which is generally more Bajan in feel. They opted to view a property in a new townhouse complex. Recently built properties on the island tend to be better constructed than older ones. Consequently, while the newer properties command higher prices, they might represent a sound investment. The property was a one-bedroomed ground-floor apartment in an extremely attractive wooden house. Its advantages were its central location within easy walking distance to the beach and various restaurants, and access to a communal pool and tennis courts. It was small, but in excellent order, and would be easy to rent immediately. Priced at £66,000, it was tempting. 'I thought it

Useful Addresses

High Commission for St Lucia
1 Collingham Gardens
London SW5 0HW
Tel: 020 7370 7123

St Lucia Tourist Board
421a Finchley Road
London NW3 6HJ
Tel: 020 7431 3675

Grenada High Commission
8 Queen Street
London W1X 7PH
Tel: 020 729 02275

Grenada Board of Tourism
1 Battersea Church Road
London SW11 3LY
Tel: 020 7771 7016

Barbados High Commission
1 Great Russell Street
London WC1B 3ND
Tel: 020 631 4975

Barbados Tourism Authority
263 Tottenham Court Road
London W1T 7LA
020 7636 0090

High Commission of the Republic of Trinidad and Tobago
42 Belgrave Square
London SW1X 8NT
Tel: 020 7245 9351

Trinidad & Tobago Tourist Office
Mitre House, 66 Abbey Road
Bush Hill Park, Enfield
Middlesex EN1 2QE
Tel: 020 8350 1009

was really sweet and loved the views, but I'd be anxious that they'd be obscured if the plot was built on,' explained Sally.

Next they went inland to see how they could get more for their money. A spacious four-bedroomed Bajan villa in the village of St Martin was on the market for £92,000. It had three reception rooms, three bathrooms, numerous patios and sun traps, plus half an acre of land with a coconut grove. It needed massive renovation but Peter was reluctant to undertake it without being on-site, although there was no doubt that with some of the dividing walls removed, the house had enormous potential. Ultimately they felt that it presented too much of a challenge.

Finally, they saw an two bedroomed, two bathroomed apartment in a quiet development in the centre of Hastings. It also had use of a communal pool and lush tropical gardens. Peter and Sally thought it was a real dream home and garden but, at £154,000, it was way beyond their budget despite the good year-round rental potential. At the time of writing, they are planning to return to Barbados to have another look at the property in Silver Sands and possibly others. They are determined to go through with their plan as a first step towards a permanent island home.

House-hunter

Right Deborah house-hunting in Tobago.

Deborah Robertson

London is a long way from Tobago in every sense, but local government manager, Deborah Robertson (known to family and friends as 'Debs'), felt it would be well worth it for regular holidays. The mortgage would be paid by letting the property at other times. 'It's virtually unspoilt, with no high-rise blocks or hotels lining the beaches, clean seas and year-round sunshine. I'd use it as a holiday home, and as I've got family in the UK, America and Jamaica, it would be a great place for us to meet up.'

The first house she saw was just outside Charlotteville, with panoramic views towards the rainforest and the sea. It had been divided into two one-bedroomed guest apartments with verandas on the ground floor, while the upper floor was an open living space. It's rare to find property in this part of the island because the locals can be reluctant to sell. As land may be owned by several members of the same family, it is worth checking exactly what you are buying. Debs was impressed. 'It's a great house in an amazing location, but unfortunately it's not quite right for me.'

Next she looked in Bacolet, a Scarborough suburb, where a two-bedroomed house designed by one of the island's leading architects was up for sale at £165,000. Resembling a white castle, it had views over the Atlantic, an airy open-plan living area and easy access to the beach, but no pool.

'I couldn't live without a pool, but I thought it was an interesting, quirky kind of house. I liked the wooden shutters and white paint, which made it feel light and fresh. I'm not sure I could work with that architecture, though – too much space is unused, so I'd need to add a new room which would require strengthened foundations and a new roof. I've got the imagination but not the cash!'

Then it was off inland to the lush farmland of the Bethel valley to look at a

A Place in the Sun

traditional Tobagan home for sale at £153,000. With three bedrooms, three bathrooms, a large wrap-around terrace, half an acre of land and spectacular views, it was certainly good value for money. 'It's nicely laid out and very spacious – the room sizes are impressive and the sea views are amazing, but it's a bit dated.' All it needed was some cosmetic work and quick action because there was already an offer on it that had not been accepted. Still undecided, Debs went to see a Georgian Caribbean-style show house in the Sanctuary Resort, a new development by Grafton beach. It had four bedrooms, three bathrooms, an open-plan reception, a private pool, tropical gardens and terraces. At £233,000, it was well over Debs' budget, but the excellent rental income could cover the cost of a mortgage. 'It is stunning with a price to match – pity it was in a location that resembled suburbia. Also, I couldn't afford it on my own.'

After much deliberation, Debs offered on the Bethel house. Her offer was accepted subject to her getting a mortgage, but since returning home, problems have arisen.

'The local banks will loan only a maximum of 70 per cent, with interest rates between 14 and 17 per cent, so I'm investigating getting one over here, but not many companies will even entertain the idea. Then I heard there's a question mark over JMC and BA flights continuing to fly there. If they stop, the remaining airline may up their prices and direct flights will be more crowded. There are also issues relating to the downturn in the US economy which may affect tourism and therefore rental potential. At the moment it feels like there are too many hurdles and I'm wondering if it's all going to be too much.'

Debs hasn't given up yet and is still investigating possible solutions, although she is wondering whether southern Europe or the hurricane-free areas of Florida may offer an easier alternative.

'It's virtually unspoilt with no high-rise blocks or hotels lining the beaches, clean seas and year-round sunshine.'

Further Reading

Specialist Books

The Daily Telegraph Guide to Living Abroad by Michael Furmell and Phillip Jones, Kogan Page, 1986.
Buying a Home Abroad by David Hampshire, Survival Books, 1998.
Live and Work in Spain and Portugal by Jonathan Packer, Vacation Work, 1998.
Buying a Home in Spain by David Hampshire, Survival Books, 2000.
Buying Property in Portugal, Portuguese Chamber of Commerce.
Buying a Home in France by David Hampshire, Survival Books, 1996.
Make Yourself at Home in France, Chambre de Commerce Française de Grande Bretagne, 2000.
The Grown-Up's Guide to Living in France by Rosanne Knorr, Ten Speed Press, 2000.
Live and Work in France by Victoria Pybus, Vacation Work, 1998.
Buying a Home in Italy by Victoria Pybus and Rachael Robinson, Survival Books, 1998.
Live and Work in Italy by Victoria Pybus, Vacation Work, 1998.
Buying a Home in Greece and Cyprus by David Walkiden, Survival Books, 2000.
Live and Work in Russia and Eastern Europe by Jonathan Packer, Vacation Work, 1998.
Buying a Home in Florida by David Hampshire, Survival Books, 1996.
Living and Working in America by David Hampshire, Survival Books, 1998.

Magazines

French Property News call 0208 543 9868 for details.
Focus on France call 01323 726040 for details.
World of Property Magazine call 01323 726040 for details.
Homes Overseas call 020 7939 9888 for details.
FT Expat call 020 8606 7545 for details.
Resident Abroad call 020 8606 7545 for details.
Spanish Homes call 020 8469 4381 for details.

General Travel Guides

The Rough Guides published by The Rough Guides.
The Lonely Planet Guides published by Lonely Planet Publications.
Thomas Cook Travellers' Guides published by Thomas Cook.
The Essential Series published by AA Books.
Eyewitness Travel Guides published by Dorling Kindersley.
Insight Guides published by APA Publications.

Property Exhibitions

Homes Overseas Exhibitions (25 exhibitions each year held in the UK, Scandinavia and Ireland) call 020 7939 9888 for details.
World of Property (three exhibitions each year in the UK) call 01323 726040 for details.

Useful Addresses

Federation of Overseas Property Developers' Agents and Consultants
95 Aldwych, London WC2B 4JF
Tel: 020 8942 0202
www.fopdac.com

Conti Financial Services
204 Church Street, Hove,
East Sussex BN3 2DJ
Tel: 01273 772811
Fax: 01273 321269
www.overseasandukfinance.com
E-Mail: enquiries @conti-financial.com

The National Association of Estate Agents
21 Jury Street, Warwick CV34 4EH
Tel: 01926 496800
www.naea.co.uk/international/overseas

John Howell & Co.
Solicitors and International Lawyers
17 Maiden Lane, Covent Garden,
London WC2E 7NL
Tel: 020 7420 0400
Fax: 020 7836 3626
www.legal21.org
E-mail: london@legal21.org
John Howell & Co is the only firm of
English solicitors to do nothing but work
involving Spain, France, Portugal & Italy.

Bennett & Co. Solicitors
144 Knutsford Road, Wilmslow,
Cheshire SK9 6JP
Tel: 01625 586937
Fax: 01625 585362
www.bennett-and-co.com
E-mail: internationallawyers@bennett-and-co.com
A specialised practice dealing in overseas
property and inheritance work in Spain,
Portugal, France, Italy, Greece, Cyprus,
Turkey, Gibraltar and the Caribbean.

Estate Agents

Spain

Marbella Homes
91 Calle Poniente, Aloha Golf, Nueva
Andalucia, 29660 Marbella, Malaga, Spain
Tel: 00 34 95 281 7107/0972
Fax: 00 34 95 281 0972
www.marbellahomes.com
E-mail: marbellahomes@hotmail.com

Viva Estates SL
C. Commercial, Reserva del Alvarito,
Urb. Andafol cn340, Km 189
29600 Marbella, Malaga, Spain
Tel: 00 34 95 283 9102
Fax:00 34 95 283 3731
www.vivaestates.com
E-mail: viva@vivaestates.com

Sunshine Estates
C. Comercial val de Pinos, Urbanisation
Calypso, 29649 Mijascosta, Malaga, Spain
Tel: 00 34 95 293 0939
Fax: 00 34 95 293 4214
www.sunshine-estates.com
sales@sunshine-estates.com

Portugal

Lammi Real Estate Agency
Avenue Fontes Pereira de Melo 3141_a&b
1050-117 Lisbon, Portugal
Tel: 00 35 121 319 3900
Fax: 00 35 121 319 3929
www.lammi.pt

Libris
Avenue Antonio Augusto
Aguiar No. 78–1 Esq,
1050-018 Lisbon, Portugal
Tel: 00 35 121 355 7755
Fax: 00 35 121 355 8855
www.libris.pt

Mar Real Estate
Estrada da Fonte Santa,
Barros de Almancil, Avia Petrol Station,
8135 Almancil, Portugal
Tel: 00 35 128 939 1491/2
Fax: 00 35 128 939 1493
www.marrealestate.co.uk

France

Alpine Apartments Agency
Hinton Manor, Eardisland, Leominster
Herefordshire HR6 9BG
Tel: 01544 388234
Fax: 01544 388 900
www.alpineapartmentsagency.com
E-mail: zigi@aaa.kcltd.co.uk

Century 21
3 rue des Cévennes, Bâtiment D,
Petite Montagne-Sud CE1701,
91017 EVRY Cedex Lisses, France
Tel: 00 33 45 54 58 995
Fax: 00 33 45 05 59 951
www.century21.fr

Arve Immobilier
20 Quai d'Arve, BP 147,
74400 Chamonix, France
Tel: 00 33 450 53 72 62
Fax: 00 33 450 53 72 25
www.arve-immobilier.com
E-mail: arve-immo@wanadoo.fr

Dauphine Rive Gauche Immobilier
24 rue Dauphine, 75006 Paris, France
Tel: 00 33 153 1011 00
Fax: 00 33 153 1011 01
www.dauphine-immo.com
E-mail: contact@dauphine-immo.com

Etudes des Voges
5 Rue du Pas du la Mole,
75004 Paris, France
Tel: 00 33 142 771 330
Fax: 00 33 142 777 722
www.etudes-voges-paris.com
E-mail: etudes.voges@free.fr

Currie French Properties
2 Fulbrooke Road, Cambridge CB3 9EE
Tel: 01223 576084
Fax: 01223 570332
E-mail: info@cfps.demon.co.uk
www.french-property.com/currie

Agence Grenaille
56 avenue de General de Gaulles, 19120
Bouleou, France
Tel: 00 33 555 91 00 30
Fax: 00 33 555 91 00 31
E-mail: Immotech@wanadoo.fr

Italy
The Best in Italy
Massilliono Ricciarini, Loc Puglia IL RIO, 17
52100 Arezzo, Italy
Tel: 00 39 0575 320 704
Fax: 00 39 0575 321331
E-mail: info@ilmeglioinitali.com

Greece
GDP Real Estate Agents
Doukos Bofor 26, 71202 Iraklion, Greece
Tel: 00 30 81 330 228
Fax: 00 30 81 281 599
www.gdp.gr
E-mail: info@gdp.gr

Paros Real Estate
Sfakion 10–12, 73100 Chania, Crete, Greece
Tel: 00 30 82 152 981
Fax: 00 30 82 156 600
www.ktimatoemporiki.gr
E-mail: info@ktimatoemporiki.gr

Euroland Crete
466 Kalives Centre, Kalives, 73003 Chania,
Crete, Greece
Tel: 00 30 82 532 557
Fax: 00 30 82 532 558
www.euroland-crete.com
E-mail: euroland@grecian.net

Euroimmo Investments
L Kountoyriotou Str. 77, 74100 Rethymno,
Crete, Greece
Tel: 00 30 83 129 685
Fax: 00 30 83 151 359
www.euroimmo.gr
E-mail: kasotakis@euroimmo.gr

Eurodome Hassapis
P Kanellopoulou No. 44,
26442 Patras, Greece
Tel: 00 30 61 429 789
Fax: 00 30 61 435 395
E-mail: eurodome@compulink.gr

Kopanitsanos Real Estate
Trade Centre (3rd floor),
40 Ermou Str., Georgiou A'Sq,
26221 Patras, Greece
Tel: 00 30 61 225 500
Fax: 00 30 61 623 923
www.estates.gr
E-mail: conkopas@otenet.gr

Pygmalion Karatzas
Andronopoulou 4, Egion,
25100 Ahaia, Greece
Tel: 00 30 69 126 801
Fax: 00 30 69 161 167
E-mail: pygmalionk@hotmail.com

Cyprus
Kolatsis Estate Agency Ltd
PO Box 57014, Limassol 3311
Cyprus
Tel: 00 357 5 342 466
Fax: 00 357 5 746 114
E-mail: Kolatsis@logos.cy.net

G. Hassapis & Sons Ltd
Gregori Afxentiou Avenue, Avencia 3
Shop 7, 6026 Larnaca, Cyprus
Tel: 00 357 4 621 130
Fax: 00 357 4 664 960
www.agora.com.cy
E-mail: Hassapis@spidernet.com.cy

Bulgaria
Real Estate Agency Atrium
66 General Kolev Street, 9002 Varna
Bulgaria
Tel: 00 359 52 25 88 01
E-mail: bgtours@ssi.bg

Kirov Real Estate Agency
Varna, Bulgaria
Tel: 00 359 52 610 391
Fax: 00 359 52 257 022

Florida
Florida Countryside
Tel: 01702 481600
www.floridacountryside.com
E-mail: enquiries@floridacountryside.com
Call or email for a free sixteen-page
brochure on buying property in Florida.

RE/MAX
29259 US Highway 19N, Clearwater
33761 Florida, USA
Tel: 00 1 727 787 4000
Fax: 00 1 727 789 1622
www.realestatetampabay.com

Sarasota Realty
438 St Armand's Circle, Sarasota
Florida, USA
Tel: 00 1 941 351 4438

Lance Donovan Real Estate
Gulfshore Square Suite 105a,
1400 Gulfshore Boulevard North
Naples, 34102 Florida, USA
Tel: 00 1 941 643 3636
Fax: 00 1 941 643 3111
www.lancedonovan.com

Bluebird Realty
26201 Hickory Boulevard, Bonita Springs
Florida, USA
Tel: 00 1 941 992 252

Prudential Florida WCI Realty
4130 Tamiami Trail North, Naples
34103 Florida, USA
Tel: 00 1 941 659 4262
Fax: 00 1 941 403 9877
E-mail: rodperson@aol.com

Coldwell Banker
3301 Del Prado Boulevard, Cape Coral
33904 Florida, USA
Tel: 00 1 941 945 1414
Fax: 00 1 941 542 9212
www.capecoral-cbms.com

Eastern Caribbean
George A Ramsay & Company Ltd
Melrose, St Thomas, Barbados, West Indies
Tel: 00 1 246 438 1376
Fax: 00 1 246 425 3053
www.ramsayrealestate.com

Terra Caribbean
The Courtyard, Hastings, Christchurch
Barbados, West Indies
Tel: 00 1 246 430 3790
Fax: 00 1 246 430 3758
www.terracaribbean.com
E-mail: wells.martin@bb.eyi.com

Abraham Tobago Realty
Bacolet Street, Scarborough, Tobago,
West Indies
Tel: 00 1 868 639 3325
Fax: 00 1 868 639 1904
www.abrahamrealty.com
E-mail: abreal@trinidad.net

Island Investments
PO Box 73, Scarborough, Tobago,
West Indies
Tel: 00 1 868 639 0929
Fax: 00 1 868 639 9050
www.isreal.com